HEART'S CRY

A DAILY JOURNEY WITH JESUS

by

Cherise Wiltshire

TABLE OF CONTENTS

Author's Note

It has been my heart's desire to write a devotional book about the wonderful journey Christ Jesus wants to take us on and to discover Him in new and exciting ways every day. This book has been a long time coming, and it was a challenging but exciting journey.

One of the greatest hindrances to me becoming a Christian was my belief that it was a boring way of living—the death of everything and anything fun. True desperation was the only reason I decided to give God a try, and even then it was begrudgingly so. Imagine then my absolute shock and amazement at the joy and wonder that was to be had in the Christian life! From the time I committed my stubborn will to God, it seemed a new lease on life was released and I was viewing life from a completely different and joyous perspective. I could see God working in my life in both small and great ways daily. All of a sudden, my burdens were no longer mine to carry but Jesus was coming into my life as my Teacher, Deliverer, Comforter, Protector, and Strength. No longer was I racing around trying to grasp happiness on the outside, but it was as if happiness was filling me up from the inside and people around me could see it too!

I have always had an affinity for writing, but I never considered writing about God initially. From the very beginning of my journey of faith, I would read online devotionals daily. A year passed with my routine until one day, my interest in doing so waned. I was perplexed! Why was I no longer interested in reading these devotionals that always encouraged me? Then I felt God's Spirit speak softly in my heart. "It is because it is time for you to start writing your own." So I began my hobby of writing encouraging words, which started about a year after becoming a Christian, and I would send them to select friends and coworkers. That was fifteen years ago.

It is my greatest desire that this book brings encouragement to you and triggers a greater passion for all that Jesus Christ has to offer. Frederick Meyer once said he "spoke words about Christ, which led me to know Him for myself." My prayer is that this book will do the same for you.

DEDICATION

This book is dedicated to the memory of Mary A. Knight, who believed in my writing long before I did. Thank you for being my encourager and for living an inspiring life of dedication to God until the very end. See you on the other side in glory.

PREFACE

With relative ease, we can get so caught up in the trappings of church, our calling, and the dos and the don'ts, that we are at risk of completely missing the boat. Christianity is essentially about getting to know the person of Jesus Christ—His work, His character, His heart, and so much more. It will take an eternity and beyond to fully grasp all of Him; and even then, there will still be more of Him to grasp! After all, the creatures have been before the throne of God for all eternity awed (Revelation 4:6–11, et al.), and every time they gaze upon Him, they still cry out in adoration and praise because they see a new facet of God that leads them to worship in reverence!

So let us take a journey to elevate our lives to a new level with God, where we no longer see Him as a far-off entity but one "who sticks closer than a brother" (Proverbs 18:24). Let us transform our lives to the place where we no longer compromise our holy calling, but instead be consumed with the reality of His holiness to such an unrelenting degree that our lifestyles reflect it as well.

Walk along the path of His love where He longs to lavish you in His loving embrace—where fears, doubts, and worries simply melt away. Climb up the mountain of faith and stand at the top, and enjoy the view with the One who will make all your cares as small as the scenery in the distance. Come aboard the flight with your Heavenly Pilot and soar to the heavenly places in your royal seat with Him.

What I don't want you to do is to read this book and take it at face value. I beseech and implore you to open your heart and spirit for God to reveal His truth for you, to have your own revelation and experience of His majestic person.

Today, your journey starts here—so turn the page and let's travel together!

ACKNOWLEDGMENTS

Writing a book takes a lot more than just an author—it takes a whole team. So permit me the opportunity to highlight those who have assisted in making this book a reality.

First, thanks to Jaqueline Inniss, my closest spiritual sister. You have been an example of grace, honesty, and integrity. You have cheered me on from the beginning. Thank you so much, my friend!

My prayer warrior, Sharon Haynes: You have been my intercessor and continued to build up my faith. Your support has been invaluable.

Special thanks to my wonderful editor, Paula Richards of Eagle Eye Editing Services, for checking in and reminding me that this book was needed when I started to doubt.

To all the team at Deep River Books for believing in my work—the warmest thanks to you all.

To my family, especially my siblings Crystal Wiltshire-Archer, and Ché and Camille Wiltshire, who have always been a steady source of honest critiques and reassurance.

To all my friends, especially Juann Carter-Brome, Jihan Greaves, Tamanika Jackson, Stephenio Abbott, Mobola Aguda, Claudia Corbin, Amanda McKenzie, Keisha and Shanelle Holford, Lana Layne-MacKie, Janelle Greenidge, Sherne Alleyne, Gertude St. John, Kiara Mendez, and Ivana Gyalogova—you all have contributed to making this book a reality, and for that I say that you each have been blessings that I wouldn't trade for anything.

A Note of Encouragement

Who do you say I am?

—Matthew 16:15

In the Gospel of Matthew Jesus asked this life-altering question of Peter, which must have been a moment pregnant with tension and purpose. To paraphrase this query: "Who am I *to you?*" Jesus Christ requires an answer to this question from each and every heart that walks this earth. Depending on who you talk to, this answer can range from a convenient swear word to "just a wise man," to "Son of God."

Jesus asked His disciples a profound question: "Who do you say I am?" Peter replied: "You are the Christ, the Son of the living God" (Matthew 16:16, ESV). Jesus replied, in essence, that Peter had answered correctly, and that on this foundational truth He would build His church. Jesus asked His disciples this question more than two thousand years ago and today, right at this divinely appointed moment in time, He is asking you the same thing: "Who do you say I am?"

We have to know Jesus in the deepest parts within us—our hearts, souls, and minds. Everything we do must come from a strong foundational knowledge of who Jesus is. It is only then that we will know who we are in Him.

The best place to find information about Jesus is to read the book about Him—the Bible. Permit me to highlight throughout this book aspects of Jesus' character to you, referencing biblical truths as the foundation.

To assist you in answering this crucial and timeless question of "Who is Jesus to you?" this book contains personal reflections of the many awesome and humbling aspects of Jesus' character, to bring us to the place of worshipping both in spirit and in truth. The Bible verses at the beginning of each devotional give you greater insight into the words that follow.

As we seek Him daily in these chapters, you will learn to reach out to Him in humility and praise for the new revelation of His Spirit. Therefore, each devotional ends with a prayer—a moment of reflection to commune with our heavenly Father, to ask by His power to make the revelation real to your heart, soul, and mind. As truth comes alive by His Spirit, a renewing of His real and powerful love will become greater. Hallelujah!

For ease of understanding, this book is broken down into four main sections. Each section begins with a short introductory summary to give the reader context for each section's purpose. The first section considers the main facets of God, to set the foundation for the majestic wonder of the Holy One. The second section focuses on how Jesus Christ relates to God as the second person of the Trinity; this section is crucial, as we need to have an unyielding understanding that Jesus Christ is the foundation of our faith and is fully God. The third section looks at some of the dimensions of Jesus. This cannot be an exhaustive list because the revelation of God is never-ending, but this section seeks to engage the reader by contemplating many of the astounding aspects of Jesus' character revealed in His Word. The fourth and final section seeks to take all the knowledge of the previous sections and lead readers to personal contemplation of how they can engage God in their everyday lives. Ultimately, it propels the reader to finally answer the question: Who is Jesus to you?

Jesus then said, "I am the one who raises the dead to life! Everyone who has faith in me will live, even if they die. And everyone who lives because of faith in me will never really die. Do you believe this?"

John 11:25–26 (CEV)

SECTION 1:

THE FACETS OF GOD

Day 1

THE FIRST STEP

You will seek me and find me when you seek me
with all your heart.

—Jeremiah 29:13

John Calvin, one of the leaders of the Protestant movement of the seventeenth century, wrote: "It is evident that man never attains to a true self-knowledge until he has previously contemplated the face of God, and come down after such contemplation to look into himself."[1] This quote is powerfully true. It brings to the fore the age-old question we have at some time or another asked ourselves: Who am I and why do I exist?

Life is a spiritual journey to find God, who is a personal Spirit and who has opened the door for us to enter His presence through Jesus' sacrifice. Jesus' wounds at the cross paid the high ransom for all sinful humans born under the curse of Adam and Eve.

Until we connect with God through His Son, life has no meaning or fulfillment. We rush around like mice in a maze, scurrying back and forth mindlessly. A couple of months before I became a Christian, I remember standing in my bedroom after a lovely day spent sailing with wonderful friends. My social life was constant. I had a fulfilling job that would be an ideal launching pad to a fast-track career to senior management. I had everything in the natural that I thought would make me happy. This had been my pinnacle of happiness, my dream to bring lasting joy.

---

[1] John Calvin, *Institutes of the Christian Religion*, Christian Classics Ethereal Library, https://www.ccel.org/ccel/calvin/institutes.html.

And yet, on that day I felt a gnawing emptiness within. Even though I was following my life plan, deep down I still felt as though I was drifting aimlessly. If all this was not making me happy, what would? I was so disgusted with the nothingness of it all that I said aloud: "If this is all there is to life, then I am not impressed."

I did not know it at the time, but my complaint was nothing new. The wisest man who ever lived, King Solomon, had the same problem, as seen in the book of Ecclesiastes. He found all the things we chase after in life as shallow and of little consequence. "I have seen all the things that are done under the sun; all of them are meaningless, a chasing after the wind" (Ecclesiastes 1:14).

Soon after, a series of events led me to the house of God, and that is where I found my fulfillment as I gave the "Jesus thing" a try. It was the epiphany I had been looking for all along and it was found in a Person. It was found in the Spirit. It was found in a Man who walked the earth many years ago. It was found in a journey I could not plan. The direction was no longer so sure that I could see it, but my heart was filled with purpose. I could not see this Person, but my heart was filled to overflowing with love, peace, and joy. I sacrificed the known for the unknown and found that the invisible was more real than the visible. I found the eternal when I turned my back on the temporal.

Such wonder began on the day I took my first step on "The Jesus Journey." Today, I am sure you are ready to do the same—so let's go!

Your Heart's Cry:

Lord, I want to seek you and find You, because You are the Way, the Truth, and the Life (John 14:6). As I embark on the devotional journey in this book, I surrender my heart and mind to Your leading and guidance in all Truth. I ask that with every devotional, You give me a better understanding of who You are and who You have created me to be. Let the light of Your countenance shine into all that I am and draw me deeper into Your everlasting love.

Day 2

GOD IS

But without faith it is impossible to please him: for he that
cometh to God must believe that he is, and that he is a
rewarder of them that diligently seek him.

—Hebrews 11:6 (KJV)

A t the most basic level of our understanding, we must believe that
God exists. "I AM WHO I AM" (Exodus 3:14) is the name God gave
to Moses before He sent him to the Israelites to free them from captivity.
This description of God speaks of a self-existing and eternal God in need
of nothing and no one. His very existence goes beyond our finite level
of comprehension, for God exists outside the constraints of time, space,
and matter. Any point of reference you use will be inadequate to fully
encompass His infinite and eternal presence.

You see, God's existence goes beyond our usual concept. When we
think of God as the eternal God, we tend to look to the future, in that
God will always exist. However, God always existed—and furthermore,
He existed *before* time. Scripture reveals that God created time as we
know it: "God called the light 'day,' and the darkness he called 'night.'
And there was evening, and there was morning—the first day" (Genesis 1:5). In the book of Revelation, when John had a vision of God,
he described the angels as saying, "Holy, holy, holy is the Lord God
Almighty, who was, and is, and is to come" (Revelation 4:8).

It is said that the descriptions John made in Revelation were so grammatically incorrect and so difficult to understand that the scholars almost
took this book out of the Bible. Some questioned if John was in his
right mind when he wrote, as some of the text seemed to not make any

sense—the above verse being one example. You see, the translators have given this verse to us as we know it today, so we can comprehend it, but when John wrote it he said that God, who was (i.e., existed in the past), at the same time is in the present, and at the very same time will already be in the future—simultaneously. Poor John couldn't find the words to explain the transcendence of God over time, so some viewed his description as gibberish.

Could you imagine having a vision of God outside the very boundaries of time? Everything we do is in reference to time, and to take away that measure makes it impossible to describe . . . anything. No wonder the words of John seemed like madness! This underscores the reality that God's existence goes infinitely beyond our limited understanding. We can never truly comprehend all that God is, for He is the Supernatural Being. Our comprehension of anything, even God, is rooted solely in our natural and limited minds. In spite of this, we must believe that He exists, even though we cannot see and touch Him as we can those around us.

Your Heart's Cry:

Lord, I believe—help my unbelief! There is so much I still need to learn about You and today is the beginning of a new journey of discovering You. I want to know You more, so I can love You more. I still have so many questions, but I am confident that You are faithful to fulfill this desire, for You promised that those who seek You will find You when they seek You with all their hearts.

Day 3

HIS GREATNESS

No one is like you, Lord; you are great, and your name is
mighty in power.

—Jeremiah 10:6

The reality is that we can never fully express the fullness of God's
nature because it is infinite in measure and its vastness extends far
beyond the natural universe.

I recall reading an article on the internet some time ago. It noted
that the distance of Earth to a certain star had been miscalculated; it had
recently been revealed that it was not, say, 25 million light years away but
only 10 million light years away. This led me to marvel at the fact that,
in relation to the distant stars, we were referring to light years. Consider
that each light year is 9.5 trillion kilometers (5.88 trillion miles). Already,
you may find it hard to process such a distance.

But wait! We then have to multiply 9.5 trillion kilometers by mil-
lions. Keep in mind that we are only talking about one star within a
relatively close solar system to ours. How about all those billions of solar
systems—those that extend toward the far reaches of the universe? Wow!
How vast the universe must be! Furthermore, God created everything—
stars, planets, and solar systems, which span beyond our comprehension.
More than that, His greatness stretches infinitely beyond the infinite universe! Just trying to wrap my mind around the size of the universe using
this light-years scale was too much for me.

In addition to all that, as the Uncreated, Self-existing Being, God
exists outside of matter, space, and time. As difficult as the vastness
described above seems, we cannot even use *that* as an accurate reference

to comprehend God's grandeur. It is just too much! God's power is absolute and all-encompassing, and He needs nothing and no one to exist. His existence is not something that can be fully comprehended by the human mind but can be accepted as divine truth, as we consider that our very existence is being suspended in the nothingness of space. It defies all logic and reason. And yet, here we are.

Your Heart's Cry:

Lord, I have looked all around, and I always find myself coming back to You. Your greatness is written in Your Word, and from beginning to end it reminds me daily of Your majesty, which goes beyond the laws of the universe. You called fire from heaven for Elijah; You fed the Israelites with manna and water in the midst of a desert; You flooded the earth and so much more. I want to see Your greatness in my life too. Open my eyes that I will see Your hand at work in my life. Let me stand in amazement and cry with rejoicing, "Great is the LORD and greatly to be praised" (Psalm 48:1, KJV)!

Day 4

His Holiness

There is no one holy like the LORD, indeed, there is no one
besides You, nor is there any rock like our God.

—1 Samuel 2:2 (NASB)

"Holiness," in its purest definition, means "separate" or "distinct."
When we refer to God's holiness, we are saying that God is distinct and separate from us at the most fundamental level. His nature is so much above ours that we can never totally comprehend it.

Every time the creatures before God's throne catch a glimpse of God, they see something so completely different and awesome that they cry out in adoration, "Holy, holy, holy is the Lord God Almighty!" They are eternally in a place of revelatory rapture for the fresh and weighty revelations of who God is. God cannot be anything but holy. We should recognize that His holiness goes well beyond the immediate thought of bright lights and flowing white robes.

God is eternal, and His holiness denotes that His very nature is absolute and his purity uncompromising. God's every intention and action is inherently pure, good, and without any form of malice or ill intent.

Holiness sets God apart from anyone or anything on a level that no one else will ever be able to attain or truly understand. Furthermore, God's dimension of holiness impacts anyone who enters into His presence. The Bible records some wonderful encounters humans have had with Him. We see in the book of Revelation that the angels fall at His feet in complete adoration, awe, and humility in His presence—keeping in mind that angels are impressive beings in and of themselves, who are loyal in their sworn allegiance to God and doing His bidding without hesitation. They are holy servants of God themselves, and humans who have encountered them found their spectacular sight so overwhelming that they were rendered speechless and scared out of their wits!

Yet as impressive as angels are, we see them in raptured, humble adoration to Someone far more impressive than themselves to a degree that they cry, "Holy, holy, holy is the Lord Almighty" (Revelation 4:8)! God's nature and His ways are worshipped without hesitancy or doubt. We can therefore appreciate that God's holiness makes God's wisdom absolutely perfect, pure, and right without doubt or question.

Your Heart's Cry:

Lord, You are truly a wonder who goes beyond my comprehension. You are holy, and I cry with the angels in adoration to You, "Holy, holy, holy is the Lord Almighty!" I want to live in awe of Your holiness, Lord. Set my eyes upon how amazing You are, and let the glory of Your presence always inspire me to seek Your presence as the deer pants for the water.

Day 5

HIS JUSTICE

Certainly the LORD is just; he rewards godly deeds. The
upright will experience his favor.

—Psalm 11:7 (NET)

"Justice" has been defined as "the quality of being just, righteous or moral uprightness,"[2] or "conformity to moral rightness in action or attitude, righteousness."[3] God is justice; He is the acceptable standard upon which we are all called to live by.

Many people find it difficult to accept this facet of God's character. They look at stories in the Old Testament and take issue with what is perceived as the unrelenting harshness of God's judgments on the people of that time. However, to look at God's decisions in such a way is too simplistic and myopic to be justified as right. One such story which reiterates this point is the experience of Job.

Here stood a man who by all accounts did not deserve to experience the series of loss, heartache, and suffering that befell him. Like many of us, Job also eventually found himself questioning God's justice. In the book, we are given the behind-the-scenes look as to why God allowed Satan to attack Job and his family with such ferocity. From such a standpoint, we usually find ourselves reading Job's complaints and getting frustrated with his long tirades as to why God's punishments were not fair. My favorite part of this book is when God replied—and Job got a revelation of God's glory. At this point, Job no longer questioned the hand of God;

---

[2] "Justice," Dictionary.com, http://www.dictionary.com/browse/justice.
[3] "Justice," The Free Dictionary, https://www.thefreedictionary.com/justice.

he seemed to have completely forgotten about his recent tragedies and the shortsightedness of focusing on God's judgment. He now understood the sovereignty of God, which had left him practically speechless. The narrow-minded view of his circumstances has dissipated to leave only the error of daring to question God's ways. He found himself repenting in awestruck wonder of God's eternal majesty.

The question of the fairness of God's justice should never only apply to those times when we fully understand His reasons for the standards or actions He takes on the earth. To understand God's justice, we must first appreciate the perfection of His knowledge. God is fully aware and understands, both at the most basic and the most complex levels, all things and how all things relate to each other. His perfect comprehension spans all dimensions in the natural and spiritual world. He perfectly understands the hearts, minds, and spirits of everyone, always. Absolutely nothing that ever was or ever will be can be hidden from God. With this in mind, we can wholly accept that God knows everything perfectly. Consequently, only He can judge anything and everything in a perfect way.

Your Heart's Cry:

Lord, knowing that You will judge justly is such a source of comfort to me. In a world where persons judge according to their own desires and plans, it is good to know that the true Judge will always see situations with perfection, impartiality, and uprightness. Today, I want to see You as Job did, and look beyond the situation of today and see You for who You are. You are the perfect judge and I accept that as the eternal truth of my heart.

Day 6

His Love

My beloved is mine and I am his.

—Song of Solomon 2:16

What is love? We all understand romantic love as displayed in countless Hollywood movies, which promote a feel-good, transient feeling towards another. May I take you a little further in our quest to understand love? Love experienced between two people encompasses commitment, trust, and an effort to know each other. Let's use these traits as a springboard to understand God's love for us.

Commitment

Love is sacrificial commitment. It requires putting the happiness and well-being of someone else above your own needs and wants. Doing this is hardly ever convenient or easy. I am sure you can think of daily scenarios where putting a loved one's needs above your own can be difficult. For a mother, it may be getting up to make breakfast for her children when she craves that extra half-an-hour in bed, or a father who would rather go golfing than the tedious Saturday chauffeuring of kids to their activities. It is the love of a partner caring for a sick loved one. Beyond such human sacrifice, God's very nature is to be committed to us to the point of sacrifice, and He exhibited this when Jesus was crucified more than two thousand years ago.

Today, He ensures that we are always welcome, no matter what. His arms of grace are always open to let us feel His eternal embrace. He wants to draw you into an intimate relationship that becomes so real, so tangible, so enlightening, it will solidify your faith beyond that of simply believing by faith but based on real experiences between you and God. A good reference of this closeness that God desires with us is stated in Psalm 91:1: "Whoever dwells in the shelter of the Most High will rest in the shadow of the Almighty." In this verse the word "dwell" means a permanent position in the presence of God.

Trust

Eventually, someone in your life will disappoint you and fail to live up to your expectation. Jesus had an appreciation for this when he walked the earth. John 2:24 (NLT) states, "But Jesus didn't trust them, because he knew human nature." God understands the limitations of humans. As well intentioned as many of us are, to put our trust completely in anyone is to set ourselves up for sure disappointment.

Herein lies the dilemma: Humans have been created to inherently trust in someone or something. Without a doubt, we all put our trust in something—be it a job, family, friends, bank accounts, entertainment, sports. You name it, someone totally trusts in it. But sooner or later, it will fail us. Because trust is a part of love, God has commanded us to "not put your trust in princes, in human beings, who cannot save" (Psalm 146:3), which means: don't depend on and love people or things so much that they are the anchors of your life. God tells us to love *Him* with all our heart, mind, body, and soul—partially to protect us from the soul-crushing disappointment that will inevitably come if we depend on anything else but Him.

Getting to Know Each Other

Before Adam and Eve sinned, we are told in Genesis that God would come down in the cool of the day to fellowship with them. Picture it: the God of the universe came from on high to talk with the first of mankind. We can imagine they sat with Him and confessed their dreams, works, and ideas in the verdant beauty of the unspoiled garden of Eden. Every day, God showed up and spent real, quality time with His cherished human creation.

Today, He is still eager to spend time with His creation. Now, as His redeemed children, He no longer comes to visit as He did in the garden of Eden. Fellowship with God has gotten even better after salvation! He dwells within us, and we can now have constant and consistent fellowship with Him whenever we want, without waiting! Oh, how He loves us!

Your Heart's Cry:

Heavenly Father, help me to be committed to You with a genuine commitment that increases daily. I want to confess everything on my heart and see You constantly work on me and the circumstances in my life for Your glory and honor. Show me more of you in unquestionable ways, every step of the way.

Day 7

HIS MERCY

Praise be to the God and Father of our Lord Jesus Christ! In his great mercy he has given us new birth into a living hope through the resurrection of Jesus Christ from the dead.

—1 Peter 1:3

Some years ago, I was earnestly seeking God because I wanted a greater revelation of who He was. The biblical descriptions were great but not personal. I wanted to have my own personal experience with Him.

One evening I was in worship when I felt a powerful presence; the atmosphere became charged and something like a heaviness filled my bedroom. A terrible fear struck me. I knew something great was going to happen, so I went on my knees and was prostrate with my face to the floor. Suddenly, I knew He was there. I looked up and it was as if the walls no longer existed or had become translucent in texture. There was a huge figure suspended above me, and as I looked toward His face all my inadequacies, my sin and weakness, become glaringly transparent. I felt unworthy and, in my heart, I cried out for forgiveness. I honestly did not think I could stay in His presence for much longer but then I looked into His eyes. At first it looked like liquid fire . . . at least that is the closest description I can give. By this time I was weeping, and my speech had suddenly disappeared; whimpers and groans were all I could manage.

At that moment, when I stared into His eyes, instead of judgment I found quite the opposite. Yes, I knew He could see all my failures, weaknesses, mistakes, and sins, but it was as if the love in His eyes covered each and every one of them. I sensed beyond any rational comprehension that His love was also covering all those failures and sins still to come.

I knew as much as I got it wrong His love was infinite and eternal and would cover them. I understood from that experience what mercy truly is. None of us deserve it.

I saw the dark, selfish wretchedness of my own soul that day and I knew my guilt could have no recompense. It was some time after that I realized my experience with God lined up with Scripture: "But the mercy and loving-kindness of the Lord are from everlasting to everlasting upon those who reverently and worshipfully fear Him" (Psalm 103:17, AMPC).

Oh, but what a wonderful God we serve who took on flesh and dwelled among us and sacrificed Himself for us—you and me!

A powerful worship singer called Misty Edwards has a song, "Tell Me What Love Is." This song expounds on what love is, and she relates love to Jesus' decision to hang on the cross to purchase the mercy of God for us. Mercy is the ultimate form of love, and for those who want it, God has given it to us all!

Your Heart's Cry:

Heavenly Father, it is humbling to see how much You loved me. You paid the ultimate sacrifice of Yourself for me. Help me to always remember that sacrificial love and live a life in honor of it. I know Your intentions for me are always good because of what You did on the cross. Your love remains for me—passionate, consistent, and eternal. Reveal Your love in my heart and fill it to overflowing. Let it flow out around me as a real-life testimony of Your unfailing love toward us all.

SECTION 2

WHO IS JESUS TO GOD?

Day 8

THE SECOND STEP

Jesus answered, "I am the way and the truth and the life. No one comes to the Father except through me."

—John 14:6

One of the most perplexing questions about Jesus is His relation to God the Father and His equality in the Trinity. This revelation is hard for even the greatest theologians to fully explain. It reinforces how far God's ways are above ours. This one eternal truth about the nature of the Trinity leaves us in total amazement. In this section I will seek to put a healthy perspective to this facet of Jesus in such a way that allows us to appreciate who Jesus is, even if we cannot completely grasp this reality.

My struggle with having a healthy, truthful outlook in relation to who Jesus is was compounded by the fact that I was raised in a religion which carries a very distorted view of Jesus. Jesus was not accepted as God but a "type of god" at best, and usually not regarded in any way close to the importance of God the Father. My journey for truth in Jesus Christ was critical to my personal growth in God. At one point, my concern for getting it wrong—coupled with what I was taught in the past, against what I was being taught as the truth at that time—became quite overwhelming. I cried out to God many times to reveal what the real truth was, and little by little I was brought to an understanding of who God is based on His Word, not distorted versions of it. Still, it was a struggle.

I cried out to God one night to help me understand the Trinity. I heard three distinct voices reply clearly: "We are one." I was later able to see how that revelation of God in my personal devotions lined up perfectly with Scripture. God is truly faithful to the faithful and to those who seek truth, He is faithful to reveal it (Jeremiah 29:13).

All of the attributes of God are found in Jesus. Hebrews 1:2–3 (KJV) speaks of "[Jesus] who made the worlds; who being the brightness of his glory and the express image of his person." He existed before the creation of the universe in perfect harmony with God the Father and God the Holy Spirit. He is the third Person that makes up the indissoluble Trinity of God.

Your Heart's Cry:

Lord, it is pivotal that I understand who You are as You have revealed Yourself in Your word. I want to be established in the eternal truth that You are God. You are the full expression of God's limitless love. In You is the fullness of life and You alone are the light of all mankind. "**For in [You, Jesus] all things were created:** *things in heaven and on earth, visible and invisible, whether thrones or powers or rulers or authorities;* **all things were created by [You] and for [You].** *[You are] before all things, and in* **[You] all things hold together**" (*Colossians 1:16–17*).

Day 9

SECOND PERSON OF THE TRINITY

"Draw near to me, hear this:
from the beginning I have not spoken in secret,
from the time it came to be I have been there."
And now the Lord GOD has sent me, and his Spirit.

—Isaiah 48:16 (ESV)

God is expressed as "one" in the Bible using the Hebrew word *echad*, which literally means "composite unity" or "unified one." So, what attributes of "Godness" does Jesus have that can help us to unequivocally and definitively know He is God?

My father used to love going to political meetings. In my youth, I could not understand why he would stand and listen for hours as the potential candidates had their say. One time he said to me, "I like to hear what a man has to say for himself." In his opinion, the words of the commentators were to be taken with a huge dose of skepticism. The tried and true test was to base the candidate on his own words.

In like manner, we can consider the words of Jesus Christ Himself the best way to consider and determine in our hearts and minds who He considered Himself to be. There is a part in the Bible that I refer to when understanding who Jesus is as it relates to His deity: "'Very truly I tell you,' Jesus answered, 'before Abraham was born, I am!' At this, they picked up stones to stone him, but Jesus hid himself, slipping away from the temple grounds" (John 8:58–59).

Another time, Jesus said to the people: "Believe me when I say that I am in the Father and the Father is in me" (John 14:11).

Finally, He said it clearly in John 10:30: "I and the Father are one."

Jesus' claim of who He is must be considered either as truth or He must be disregarded completely as an outright liar and deceiver or a madman. Why? Because those statements He made to the Jews at the time made it clear that He was in equal standing with God and that He existed hundreds of years before Abraham, who was seen as the founding father of the Jewish faith. He calls God His Father and refers to Himself as His Son. All of this we would accept today, but back in the time when Jesus walked the earth, this type of talk was considered blasphemous and insulting to God, and as a result the people tried to seize him to punish him.

Jesus gave a clear account of who He was, is, and always will be. We all have to make the decision to take Jesus at His word. It is as simple as that.

Your Heart's Cry:

Lord, everyone in this world has their own opinions of who You are, but I choose to take You at Your word. You have given a clear description of who You are, and today I set my heart to accept and live in that truth. I trust that You will lead me to know this truth to be real, as You reveal who You are in my day-to-day walk with You. In this I will trust.

Day 10

THE WORD

He sent out his word and healed them; he rescued
them from the grave.

—Psalm 107:20

The word "role" means an expected behavior or job a person possesses or acts. First John 2:1 indicates that Jesus' role within the Trinity is a "speaking role." This corresponds to Genesis 1 where speaking was crucial to creation being formed: 'God said [spoke] . . ." (Genesis 1:3, et al.). Jesus then, is the Spoken Word. The book of Revelation calls Him this name as well: "He is dressed in a robe dipped in blood, and *his name is the Word of God*" (Revelation 19:13, emphasis added).

Furthermore, we know that God is Spirit and invisible, having no physical form, so we cannot truly behold Him as He is. Jesus, however, is "the visible image of the invisible God" (Colossians 1:15, NLT). Jesus gave substance, dimension, and physicality to God so that we can behold Him at our human level.

The word *logos* would be defined today by ancient Jewish and Greek standards of interpretation as "an instrument for the execution of God's will," i.e., the personification of God's revelation. To the Greeks specifically, *logos* was thought of as a bridge between the transcendent God and the material universe. Both provide an excellent description of Jesus' role; the Jews understood the Word to be a person who reveals God, and the Greeks understood the Word to be a mediator between God and man. Both are correct as shown in John 14:9, when Jesus tells his disciples: "Anyone who has seen me has seen the Father."

The book of Psalms also foretold Jesus' role when it says, "He [God] sent his word [Jesus] and healed them; he rescued them from the grave" (Psalm 107:20). Jesus as the Word is shown to be the One sent to provide salvation to mankind.

Another dimension of Jesus' role is that He is the foundation upon which our faith must rest. The Bible tells us, "faith comes from hearing the message, and the message is heard through the word about Christ" (Romans 10:17). Jesus Christ, the Word, presents Himself to us, and upon Him our faith blossoms and grows as He continuously reveals more of Himself over the courses of our lives.

Your Heart's Cry:

Heavenly Father, Jesus is the Word who became flesh and dwelt among us. He spoke Your eternal truth for us to know You and to live according to Your royal way. Thank You for revealing Your Word that truly brings life to our hearts and minds. Thank You for Your word that renews our minds to be like Christ. I am excited and willing to continue to allow the Word to transform me into the best version of me You intended me to be.

Day 11

ONE WITH THE FATHER

But Jesus remained silent and gave no answer.
Again the high priest asked him, "Are you the Christ,
the Son of the Blessed One?"

"I am," said Jesus. "And you will see the Son of Man
sitting at the right hand of the Mighty One and coming
on the clouds of heaven."

—Mark 14:61–62

Jesus was a man who could command the powers of heaven, destroy the works of hell, and soften the hardest hearts. Jesus stands out in the chapters of time, and to this day we still use BC and AD to denote the centuries. It is as if even time itself would acknowledge Jesus' time on earth as forever distinguishing the time that preceded Him and the time that followed His resurrection. No doubt, we can all agree that He was truly a great man with divine powers and revelation. But was He so divine as to be considered one with God?

This has been debated fiercely throughout the ages. Several religions choose to acknowledge Jesus as a prophet or a great wise and spiritual man, but only Christianity contends that He is one with the Father. From the very onset of Jesus' ministry, there were constant queries and demands for Jesus' identity to be made clear in relation to his relationship with God. Jesus Christ was the human representation of the invisible God. He came to the earth in human form by divine conception to fulfill the many prophecies foretold by the Old Testament prophets and to reconcile humans back to God. He purchased mercy by being the sacrifice for our sins. The understanding that Jesus Christ who walked the earth as man and the God of the universe are one and the same is a very confusing concept, as the human mind cannot comprehend how a Person can be a part of something as one but can exist completely separate to it.

The truth is, nothing is better at explaining Jesus than the book written about Him, the Bible. John 14:7–11 (NKJV) notes:

"If you had known Me, you would have known My Father also; and from now on you know Him and have seen Him."

Philip said to Him, "Lord, show us the Father, and it is sufficient for us."

Jesus said to him, "Have I been with you so long, and yet you have not known Me, Philip? He who has seen Me has seen the Father; so how can you say, 'Show us the Father'? Do you not believe that I am in the Father, and the Father in Me? The words that I speak to you I do not speak on My own authority; but the Father who dwells in Me does the works. Believe Me that I am in the Father and the Father in Me, or else believe Me for the sake of the works themselves."

Aren't these words absolutely amazing when you sit and carefully consider them? Jesus is clearly stating that His existence is not separate from God but that there is no difference between Himself and God. It fits perfectly with what the apostle John said: "The Word [Jesus] was God" (John 1:1).

Once again, we can be confident that Jesus and the Father are one based on Jesus' own words. What more could we ever need after reading these words of truth from the Word of truth?

Your Heart's Cry:

Heavenly Father, how blessed are we that You have revealed the truth of Your Son to us. We accept that Jesus and You are One as Jesus revealed when He walked the earth. My God, let this truth not just stay as head knowledge, but let it be cemented to my core so that I will be established forever in truth and guided by that truth through Your Spirit all the days of my life. Thank You for the freedom of truth; may I never take it for granted.

Day 12

THE SON OF GOD

After Jesus said this, he looked toward heaven and prayed:
"Father, the time has come. Glorify your Son, that your
Son may glorify you."

—John 17:1

In secondary school, I had a Muslim friend by the name of Hasena. Now Hasena and I were very good friends and she was extremely devoted to her faith. Inevitably, religion would come up in our discussions. Now, keep in mind, I had very little understanding about Jesus or what the Bible said about Him. All I knew was that you said the Lord's Prayer at assembly every day, sang some boring hymns, and learned some psalms. I had yet to truly understand the fundamentals of faith; have any real, personal encounter with God; or study His Word. I remember distinctly saying, as we were sitting in chemistry class one afternoon, "I can feel Christmas in the air." To which she replied she felt nothing, and that Christmas meant nothing to her. She went on to say, "How can you believe that Jesus is the Son of God? How can God have a son? That is so impossible that God could come into the earth through a woman! That is too stupid to believe and yet you all still believe it!"

When she said that, I asked: "Don't you believe in Jesus?" She replied: "Sure, we see him as a great teacher, and he is even in our Qu'ran. But to believe he is the Son of God? Of course not; that is crazy!"

At that time, I had little to offer in the way of defending the truth because I did not really know the truth myself. Furthermore, she was successful in causing me to doubt. Was I stupid to accept that Jesus Christ was the Son of God, born of a virgin in the town of Bethlehem? Could it be that all along I had been deceived? I worried over this for some time.

What Hasena failed to understand was that God is not limited to our understanding when He chooses to act. His supernatural ways will not always conform to our rational minds, and that is great—despite our limited powers of reason, Jesus was able to come and save us all and give eternal life! I don't know about you, but I would rather be saved without understanding than not be saved. God did a miracle by sending Jesus into the earth—it was a wondrous act from a wondrous God. That I can definitely accept!

I am so grateful that God led me to His truth, and now I know why Jesus being accepted as the Son of God has stood the test of time, in spite of so many who discredit him. His truth lives on! Hallelujah!

Your Heart's Cry:

Lord, thank You for revealing the truth of who You are to me; You are the Son of God. I bring those who still live in darkness and don't know this truth to You, and I intercede on their behalf. I pray the light of Your truth will also be revealed to them—that they will know that You alone are the Truth, the Way, and the Life. I pray that each person will know You as their personal Savior and live the rest of their lives in adoration and praise to You, Jesus Christ, Son of the Living God.

Day 13

THE POWER AND WISDOM
OF GOD

*... but to those whom God has called, both Jews and
Greeks, Christ the power of God and the wisdom of God.*

—1 Corinthians 1:24

Some consider Jesus to be the Savior but do not accept that He also provides to us access to the power and wisdom of God. Jesus died for our salvation and rose again, and we know He sits at the right hand of the Father.

Jesus said that if we ask anything in His name it would be given to us. Do you know why He made this promise to us? Because we must be reminded that it is by His name that we can draw upon all the power and wisdom of God to live a victorious life!

The goodness of Jesus did not end when He returned to heaven. His divine provision is still extended to us today. Jesus still wants to reveal all of who He is to each one of us personally every single day. He wants us to come and ask for His power to see miracles occur all around us, just as when He walked the earth.

Let us not settle for less than God's best in our lives. Jesus wants to fill us to overflowing with His knowledge and power. James 3:17–18 reminds us: "the wisdom that comes from heaven is first of all pure; then peace-loving, considerate, submissive, full of mercy and good fruit, impartial and sincere." Open your heart and mind to receive this truth, and let Christ Jesus reveal this eternal truth in your life from today onward!

Your Heart's Cry:

Heavenly Father, You have made Your wisdom and power available to all who believe in You. I ask for the attributes to manifest in my life from today. I accept that only You see the end from the beginning. Only You see all the variables I can't know. Only You have the power to work everything out for my good and Your glory. I humbly welcome this divine phenomenon into my heart and mind and surrender to Your mighty hand.

SECTION 3

THE DIMENSIONS OF JESUS

Day 14

THE THIRD STEP

In [Jesus] was life, and that light was the light
of all mankind.

—John 1:4

Having a healthy vision and understanding of who Jesus really is will be a deciding factor in how successful our Christian growth will be. We are called to be in constant fellowship with Him, and our concept of Him will either encourage or discourage us to be in His presence, "because as [Jesus] is, so are we in this world" (1 John 4:17, KJV). As God's beloved, we are to focus on Jesus' nature and by doing so, we naturally become like Him. The importance of this truth cannot be emphasized enough.

Once we focus on the person who is our Messiah, Jesus Christ, and continue to improve and increase in our knowledge of Him, our spiritual experience and growth will increase exponentially. An exciting, God-filled life will be the result, and you will wonder why you stayed in the shallow end of God's grace for so long when infinite wonders of His person were at your fingertips waiting to be discovered!

Allow me the awesome privilege of giving you a taste of those wonders in the pages to come.

Your Heart's Cry:

Heavenly Father, You have made available to us the gift that is Jesus Christ. The same Person who spoke the world into existence is now our own, and He is ours! Jesus is the Living Word who penetrates even to dividing soul and spirit and judges the thoughts and attitudes of the heart (Hebrews 4:12). Lord, let me know You more through Your word so I can follow Your royal ways and live in Your presence. Reveal to me Your Son Jesus with increasing understanding, and fashion me to be like Him so I can show You to the world through my submission to Your ways.

Day 15

HIS HUMANITY

[Jesus] became flesh and dwelt among us

—John 1:14 (ESV)

Many times, when we think of Jesus Christ, we separate Him from our own reality to the point where He seems so disconnected from us using our own perception. So much so that we leave no room for an authentic relationship in our distant vision of His grandeur.

In this way of thinking, we have disregarded the humanness of God when He walked on earth. In contrast, by accepting the fact that He became one of us, it becomes possible for us to expect Jesus to relate with our sufferings, struggles, and weaknesses. God understands our frailties in a way that only one who has also lived it can. This realization gives us a more balanced perspective and frees us from embarrassment, fear, and judgment, allowing us to comfortably approach Him with any of our thoughts, cares, or concerns.

Do you speak to your boss with the same affection and unabashed rapport that you do with a friend? Most persons would answer no, because the perception of a boss brings a certain formality and distance which establishes a huge difference in the two relationships. Or, have you ever spoken with someone and at some point either you or the other person says: "You aren't in my situation; you wouldn't understand"? As much as we would hate admitting it, this person is usually right. Unless you have experienced the same situation, it is difficult to fully relate to the person's problem.

Jesus' time on earth was not without encounters of temptation, betrayal, abandonment, rejection, loneliness, distrust, envy, jealousy, hatred, greed, hypocrisy, and ultimately torture unto death. The Bible calls Him "a Man of sorrows" (Isaiah 53:3, NJKV). Seeing Jesus as one who understands our every experience is important, because to do so opens up the possibility of a relationship which cannot be matched.

Understanding His human experience does not belittle the "Godness" of our Lord, but it does make Him more approachable because we know He has already been through similar issues. Just like you, He has been there. He has experienced "that," whatever it may be, since He experienced the worst the world has to offer. So when we think to approach Him, burdened by the tragedies, frailties, and worries of life, His heart is full of compassion and understanding.

Today, go before Him, understanding that He has walked a very similar road. He is right by your side, waiting to hold your hand and guide you through it.

Your Heart's Cry:

Heavenly Father, knowing that Jesus was afflicted and knew the anguish this fallen world can bring is a constant source of reassurance to me. I know that He understands my fears and trials because He was once there too. I know that His eyes are on me with compassion because He truly fellowships in my sufferings. Today, I bring all those burdens before You with an open and confident heart. Thank You for listening to all my concerns with the understanding of being there.

Day 16

HE OVERCAME SIN

For we do not have a high priest who is unable to empathize
with our weaknesses, but we have one who has been tempted
in every way, just as we are—yet he did not sin.

—Hebrews 4:15

A lot of people mistakenly believe that Jesus was sinless simply because
He had the power of God. But to believe this would not only be
grossly untrue but neutralize the purpose and impact of His life here on
earth. Why? Because Jesus had to conquer sin in a human body, in order
to fulfill the righteous requirement humanity needed to be the perfect
and spotless lamb of God (2 Corinthians 5:21; 1 Peter 1:19).

Could Jesus existing in a godly state be the perfect sacrifice? No! The
Bible states that it had to be a human sacrifice, and so Jesus had to be in
all aspects human even in His decision not to sin.

Jesus' triumph over sin was revealed when He was tempted in the
desert for forty days by the Devil (Matthew 4:1–11). The Devil tried
three times to get Jesus to sin by appealing to three of the most basic
aspects of human nature: lust of the flesh, pride, and lust of the eyes.

Righteousness is to know what is right or wrong and choose to do
right consistently— i.e., knowing what is God's will against what isn't—
and then choosing God's will every time. Jesus Christ, in His complete
humanness, chose at all times to make God's will His way to follow.

Now, since Jesus has fulfilled the righteous requirement and became
the perfect sacrifice, He has conquered and destroyed the power of sin
over us. So because He has become victorious, we have the power through
Him to be victorious as well.

Today, choose to rely on His power to conquer sin in your life. His power is the only way to be victorious. He provided that power when He died on the cross and was resurrected three days later. You have the victory in Jesus Christ, so access that victory today!

Your Heart's Cry:

Heavenly Father, Jesus lived a pure and sinless life when He walked the earth. He did it to be an acceptable sacrifice for my salvation. When I consider that Jesus fulfilled the righteous requirement by overcoming sin for us—which means that I too can be free from my own bondage to sin—I am left in awe of Your grace. Jesus has overcome the power of sin, and from today I walk in freedom because sin no longer has dominion over me.

Day 17

THE PERFECT MODEL

I have set you an example that you should do as
I have done for you.

—John 13:15

Jesus Christ stands alone in the annals of human history. As a man, He experienced the pain, sadness, loneliness, betrayal, abandonment, and suffering that so many of us have experienced, yet never succumbed to temptation. He never took the easy way out or the path of least resistance. Keep in mind that Jesus could have lived a life of comfort and relative peace in the Jewish community if He had so desired. However, He made it his mission to go to the diseased, suffering, and lost to deliver them from their bondage. He submitted to the will of the Father to endure the pain of the cross and all its related suffering, to see God's will for humanity fulfilled, and destroy the works of the enemy. He walked the narrow road of love, mercy, holiness, grace, and truth like no other ever had before (Matthew 7:14).

The standard He set is an important one for those who have accepted His sacrifice and chosen to submit their lives to God's divine will. His life is the level to which each and every one of us must seek to attain. "So, my dear Christian friends, companions in following this call to the heights, take a good hard look at Jesus. He's the centerpiece of everything we believe, faithful in everything God gave him to do" (Hebrews 3:1–6, MSG).

Jesus is the visible image of the invisible God. How did Jesus display His deity while in human form? He showed mercy to the adulterous woman (John 8:3), forgiveness of sins (Matthew 26:28), fed the hungry

(Luke 3:11), loved the "unworthy" (John 4:5-42), spread the good news (Mark 16:15), delivered the captives oppressed by the Devil (Luke 4:18), and healed diseases (Mark 1:34).

Your Heart's Cry:

Dear Heavenly Father, You have set a perfect example of how to live a victorious life on this earth. You are the Living Word. You have called me to follow the model and I really want to do so. Let your grace strengthen me to achieve this every day by opening my eyes to the opportunities to display Christ in my vocation and all the other places and people You would lead me to. I want to be authentic in my devotion to You. I don't want to display a surface-level obedience and not a genuine heartfelt commitment to Your way. In the private and public places, let my life-style consistently represent Your love and holiness.

Day 18

THE SPOTLESS LAMB

For Christ also died for sins once for all, the just for the
unjust, so that He might bring us to God, having been put to
death in the flesh, but made alive in the spirit.

—1 Peter 3:18 (NASB)

God knows how to set the stage and plot for a marvelous reveal.
When watching a movie with a well-written script, you enjoy the
plot more when a little nugget of truth is revealed as the story develops. It
hardly seems significant at the time, but as the full truth is revealed in the
end, the surprise is usually an "aha moment," bringing much satisfaction
to the viewer. Usually, in the final scenes when all is revealed, they will
give a flashback or series of flashbacks to shed light on the little clues that
were glimpsed at strategic points in the movie.

Similarly, but on an infinitely bigger scale, God wrote the script of
this age before time existed. In the first act we call the Old Testament,
priceless clues are littered like Hansel and Gretel's trail of breadcrumbs—
toward the truth that was only fully revealed when Jesus died and was
resurrected.

You see, the Old Testament way of cleansing sin was to bring a lamb
without blemish to be sacrificed as an offering to God for the forgiveness
of sins (Exodus 12:5; Leviticus 1:3; 22:19–24). This was the foreshadow-
ing of what was to come. We know that we have all sinned and fallen
short of God's glorious standard (Romans 3:23), and I believe we would
have continued to fall woefully short if not for the Spotless Lamb who
was slain for our transgressions. Upon this backdrop we can ask the question: Why was Jesus the sacrifice?

Anyone born of both a man and a woman are automatically sinful, as descendants of Adam and Eve. Because of this, no human could be spotless (i.e., sinless) to be the sacrifice for humanity's rebellion against God. But here is the catch-22: neither an angel nor an animal (like a lamb) could fulfill the requirement either. Only a human could be the sacrifice for humanity's sin. But God wrote the script, and He had a big reveal coming in act two: the New Testament.

Jesus came into the earth in human form born of a virgin (Isaiah 7:14) and was subject to all this fallen world had to offer: temptation, loss, sickness, hunger, disease, selfishness, greed, betrayal, and hopelessness, to name a few. And yet He chose within His human frailty not to sin. It is important to note this fact; He was not only born sinless but chose to live a sinless life on the earth. At the time of His crucifixion, then, Jesus was worthy to be the spotless (sinless) sacrifice and the real spotless lamb, fulfilling the prophecy of the Old Testament.

Your Heart's Cry:

Heavenly Father, You truly are the greatest scriptwriter of all time. Just when the world was destined toward a hopeless end, You provided the perfect plot twist and provided a Savior for us all! We now can take comfort that in You we are now destined for a happy ending: eternal life in Your Presence. Thank You for Your willingness to come into this earth—a hopeless world we created in disobedience—and to provide the way of escape.

Day 19

THE HEART OF COMPASSION

When He went ashore, He saw a large crowd, and felt compassion for them and healed their sick.

—Matthew 14:14 (NASB)

J esus did not put on a front; He was genuinely compassionate when
He walked the earth in human form. He was the most compassionate of men, and we can say this with confidence because several times in
the Gospels it says He was moved with compassion. This heart of compassion led Him to connect with the pain and needs of the people He
encountered, and He followed it up with action. His sympathy for their
fallen state led Him to perform actions of love. After He felt the pain and
hopelessness of the person, He tapped into His divine power to right the
wrong existing in their lives. In every instance in the Gospels, we saw this
being played out—whether with a crowd of hungry people; the blind,
deaf and lame; a widow mourning her only son; or a lonely tax collector
starved for love and acceptance. Jesus felt and met the desperate need for
each of them personally, and answered the desires of their hearts.

First and foremost, Jesus always identified and felt their suffering. He
was willing to come alongside the suffering as closely as He could. He
was not distant in His interactions with the people; His was a personal
attention and care. We can understand why 1 Corinthians 13 makes it
so emphatically clear that if what we do doesn't come from a place of
authentic care and affection for those around us, we can consider our
efforts as wasted.

As we read the Gospels' recount of His life, we see that Jesus modeled
real compassion for us. That model is what we have been called to follow.

The Holy Spirit has been sent to every believer, to give us the ability to become just as compassionate as Jesus was when He lived on the earth. That same desire to see people delivered from their afflictions, living with the truth of God's love and secure in His power, is what He has called us to have as His ambassadors in the earth.

Your Heart's Cry:

Precious Lord, You have provided the perfect model of compassion to us. It is the same thing I want to be made evident in my life on a daily basis. Fill me with Your love to overflowing each day, so that I can go into the world and share in abundance the love overflowing in my heart to so many who need it. Reveal to me in my day-to-day life where You want me to reach out and bring real transformation of Your peace, love, and joy to those I encounter. Let each person I reach point straight to You. Let it be always for Your glory and honor, and let Your name be lifted up as the true Comforter and Provider. This is my prayer, Lord; answer me by Your grace.

Day 20

THE SOVEREIGN KING

Would not his splendor terrify you? Would not the dread of
him fall on you?

—Job 13:11

The Jews wanted to put Jesus on an earthly throne. They thought
He was the Messiah, but they did not understand that His purpose
went far beyond their temporal needs and desires.

You see, the Jewish people wanted the prophesied Messiah to liber-
ate them from Roman domination. Jesus refused to allow their desires to
negate the real purpose for Him coming to the earth. He said to Pontius
Pilate "My kingdom is not of this world" (John 18:36). Jesus Christ rules
over the entire universe. The word "sovereign" means that He has divine
rulership over everything. His is total and absolute power. His reign is
infinite in space, matter, and time.

Having a healthy and honest understanding of God's greatness is
the basis upon which reverential awe is activated. We may even become
overwhelmed at this reality—for if He is sovereign, we really have little
control, right? Even in His power, Jesus "is light; in him is no darkness"
(1 John 1:5). With all His power, He wants to use it in our lives for our
good and the good of the world.

In the Chronicles of Narnia, there is a conversation during which
one of the children asks Mr. Beaver about the lion, Aslan. Aslan was a
mythical representation of Jesus Christ in the book. The child, Susan,
asked if Aslan was safe, because she would feel nervous about meeting a
lion. To which Mr. Beaver remarked that Aslan was not safe, but he was
good—because he was the king.

Jesus truly is the Good King. He is not safe, but He is good. This is in keeping with the apostle John's revelation in the book of Revelation. Here was a man who was arguably the closest disciple to Jesus, the one who knew Jesus on a real and personal level as He walked this earth. Yet, when he saw Jesus Christ in all His glory, he did not relate to Him in the same way he would have when He was on earth. Why? After all, He was the same Jesus he had known for several years on earth.

John's reaction to Jesus changed because Jesus' image had changed. He was no longer a gifted teacher, powerful prophet, or miracle healer. He was no longer just a best friend. He was the great and all-powerful King of heaven, reigning in unimaginable glory. John reacted to Him as the King He was and is and always will be. Reverential awe was John's response. What is yours?

Your Heart's Cry:

Dear Lord, You are truly good and loving in all You do but Jesus, never let me forget that You are the King of heaven. Let me never regard You with anything less than the reverential awe You deserve. Let me worship You gloriously like the angels of heaven do. Let me cast away all my cares like the crowns the elders lay at Your feet, to give You the adoration You command. In that place, I will see You high and lifted up and I will see You more clearly. In that place, I will know You as the great King You are.

Day 21

THE PERFECT SERVANT

For even the Son of Man came not to be served but to serve,
and to give his life as a ransom for many.

—Mark 10:45 (ESV)

We who are God's beloved serve a very "strange" king—at least by society's standards! He chose to wash feet, heal the rejected, make friends with the lowest of society, and die for people who wished Him crucified. A strange kind indeed! More than that, He calls us to do the same: love the unlovable, serve the outcasts, make friends with the rejected, and bless those who persecute us. He became the perfect servant to show us the path to follow. Our hearts, once connected to God, will cry out for ways to serve.

Jesus came from heaven to live as a human and to die for the sins of mankind, so that man would have an opportunity to be reconciled to God and not suffer God's judgment. Jesus laid aside His glory to come to a fallen world. Jesus the Ruler became the servant for an unworthy and rebellious race. Jesus, who created everything, allowed Himself to suffer under what He created to fulfill divine purpose.

God chose to become man for thirty-three years to give all men eternity, but the serving does not end there. Jesus continues to pray for us unceasingly before our Father in heaven. Romans 8:34 (NLT) says: "Who then will condemn us? No one—for Christ Jesus died for us and was raised to life for us, and he is sitting in the place of honor at God's right hand, pleading for us."

Against this backdrop, what service has God called you to? Have you scoffed at it and said it was too much of a sacrifice or below your status?

Let me remind you of what was stated in God's Word: "he made himself nothing" (Philippians 2:7). If the God of the universe could put away all His status and all His glory for you, then surely you can put away your pride and see the honor in servanthood.

The early church was known for its servanthood. So much so, that history records a letter from a town leader who mentioned the service of the Christians. He said because of them there were no beggars to be found; the Christians took care of the elderly and assisted the poor. He praised them for their actions—and he was an unbeliever!

The truth, as strange as it may seem, is this: "The greatest among you will be your servant" (Matthew 23:11). Starting today, let us put away the lie that serving makes our value less. In God's eyes, it is a position of honor, which He Himself carried for us, even until death.

Your Heart's Cry:

Heavenly Father, I want to have the heart of a servant. To serve is to honor You, and that is my deepest desire. Let me live as Christ in my actions of service. Reveal to me the ways I can be of assistance in every area of my life. Increase my desire for this role and let humility be the hallmark of all I do. May Your goodness in me be displayed from today onward.

Day 22

THE PREEMINENT PROFESSOR

Anyone who goes too far and does not abide in the teaching of Christ, does not have God; the one who abides in the teaching, he has both the Father and the Son.

—2 John 1:9 (NASB)

The Sermon on the Mount was a powerful teaching message that can be easily misinterpreted by the undiscerning, and the truth of Jesus' revelation lost (Matthew 5:1–8). It is my belief that studying this sermon is important to understanding who Jesus was and what He was calling each of those listening to become.

"Blessed are the poor in spirit": This speaks of each person admitting that they cannot gain any real spirituality without God. There are many who claim to be spiritual, using eloquent words to justify what really is self-idolization, the belief that "within me I have everything to be right, good, and true." We who see Christ as our Savior perceive spirituality as "I can do absolutely nothing right, good, or true without God."

"Blessed are those who mourn": On the surface, this passage seems to be referring to death, but upon greater consideration Jesus was really referring to something far beyond mourning for a deceased loved one. Here, He was referring to those who not only realize the deficiency in their dormant spiritual condition but who desperately want to change it. They cry out to God for radical change within them. Their need is so great that Jesus alluded to their yearning as those who yearn after those they have lost. Is this you? Today, have you cried out to God for a change from your current spiritual reality for more of His glory, more of His nature being revealed in you? We must never get complacent, thinking we have arrived; we must always be mourning, yearning and aching for more of God in our lives.

"Blessed are the meek": When I hear the word "meekness," I am always tempted to think that this represents a wimpy, self-conscious, weak person—a pushover who never speaks up or stands for anything, a person just scurrying around in the shadows. However, such a depiction is the exact opposite of the truth. We know this because Jesus acted out meekness—and it was anything but what I just described. Jesus was bold to tell the truth but always did it with gentleness, coming from a place of love. Meekness does not mean a lack of self-confidence but confidence with self-control. Each of us has been called to speak the truth and live it authentically, not with undue force or aggression but with a kindness and love in our speech and uprightness in our actions. The meek never vie for the spotlight, but allow their lifestyle and God's Spirit to bring people to inquire of truth from them.

"Blessed are those who hunger and thirst for righteousness": If you have ever experienced extreme thirst or hunger, you know how desperate you are to have the need filled. A person usually can't see past that need because it is so consuming. Our spiritual need has to be the same. Certainly, we all have a tendency to put our spiritual needs as the last ones on our to-do lists. But in reality, we really need to make them our primary focus. You see, we have to desperately want something in order to go to all lengths to get it. It makes sense then that the Bible says: "For He has satisfied the thirsty soul, and the hungry soul He has filled with what is good" (Psalm 107:9, NASB).

"Blessed are the merciful": More often than not, our first response is to condemn a person for wrongdoing; but when the tables are turned, we tend to excuse our oversights and mistakes. God is perfect in all His ways, yet He extends mercy to us countless times. How much more should we, in our imperfections, extend that same mercy to others? Jesus responded to Peter's question on the number of times to forgive another by saying this: "I tell you, not seven times, but seventy-seven times" (Matthew 18:22).

"Blessed are the pure in heart": This speaks of a person who comes to God unmasked, rather than hiding behind achievement, self-righteousness, or any other walls to keep from God. This may seem silly, but many of us do this. I remember watching a talk show, and a guest was making excuses with highly intellectual jargon to justify an obvious problem in his life. The host very quickly saw past all the façade and zeroed in on the problem, stating clearly what it was.

Jesus was trying to get people to be genuine with God about their true state. God cannot help a person who is in denial. The Pharisees were a classic case. They had all the intellectual words, position, and power. Most seemed to have self-righteousness coming out of their ears! And you know what? Jesus could not help them. Their masks were firmly in place and so deeply embedded that they refused to pull them off to acknowledge truth, let alone apply it to their lives. What a tragedy!

God can help you overcome any problems you may have. However, this is conditional on your honesty. Jesus plainly said that He came for the sick. He came because all of us are spiritually sick and need help in getting back to optimal spiritual health. Let us all go for our daily check-ups and receive the medicine to cleanse, repair, and restore our beings to the wholeness and beauty God intended. Now that is never a pill too hard to swallow!

Your Heart's Cry:

Heavenly Father, You truly are the greatest teacher who has ever walked this earth. As the Sermon on the Mount shows, Your wisdom is eternal and true. Your teaching is not for the faint of heart, but I am confident You will provide me with the grace to be one who is poor in spirit, mourns, is meek, hungers and thirsts for righteousness, and is merciful and pure in heart. Let me not stay in the shallow waters of my faith; challenge me to go deeper in You, so I can truly reflect Your nature to the world as a testimony of You.

Day 23

THE HIGH PRIEST

Therefore he is able to save completely those who come to
God through him, because he always lives to intercede
for them.

—Hebrews 7:25

One of the most poignant prayers Jesus prayed was in the garden of Gethsemane. Even as He prayed for Himself, it was always from a place of selflessness—fulfilling the mandate of God. His words "Not my will but your will be done" should echo in our hearts and minds daily.

Furthermore, John 17:21–23 shows Jesus praying on behalf of the church: "that all of them [believers] may be one, Father, just as you are in me and I am in you. May they also be in us so that the world may believe that you have sent me. I have given them the glory that you gave me, that they may be one as we are one. . . . Then the world will know that you sent me and have loved them even as you have loved me."

Jesus still prays for God's glory to be revealed in our lives today. He prays for all the hard times we will inevitably face, for God's strength and grace to see us through. He prays that our faith will be strengthened to believe God for the impossible. He prays that we will not lose sight of the higher calling—to seek, know, and obey God. He prays for all those who still exist in darkness to come into His marvelous light. He prays for the poor and disadvantaged to be provided for. He prays for our hearts to be filled with compassion to reach out to those unfortunate souls. He prays that we will not live a life of limitations but will continue to press on to greater glory and to manifest His greatness in our lives.

He is constantly praying for us and we call this type of prayer intercession. Intercession simply means making an earnest request to God for His power to bring protection, breakthrough, provision or any other type of holy intervention for the person or persons being prayed for. Jesus Christ intercedes for us; He petitions our heavenly Father, giving utterance to our needs that we sometimes can't put into words—at times when our hearts are so heavy we can only groan and moan in grief and desolation. Thankfully, Jesus translates those unintelligible yearnings into petitions before His Father for each of us. When our will and our flesh grow weak, there He kneels, praying for each of us to be sustained.

We can once again see the power of His prayer in Gethsemane when the angel came and tended to Him. Jesus understood that He needed the strength of His heavenly Father to go through the suffering He was asked to bear. When you realize that you are in a difficult position, do you do the same? Do you go to God and seek His help to see you through?

Your Heart's Cry:

Lord, let me never forget that You are always before the throne of the Father, praying for me. I have such reassurance that Your intercession means I am always on Your heart and mind. There is endless comfort in my heart knowing that You hear my every dream and wish, and that You are faithful to see my sincere desires fulfilled. In my weakness You ensure that I am strengthened to continue in good works. In my sin, You freely forgive and sanctify me. I accept the blessings that Your intercession brings, Lord. With all that I am, I thank You.

SECTION 4

WHO IS JESUS TO YOU?

Day 24

THE FOURTH STEP

Therefore, I urge you, brothers and sisters, in view of God's
mercy, to offer your bodies as a living sacrifice, holy and
pleasing to God—this is your true and proper worship.
Do not conform to the pattern of this world, but be
transformed by the renewing of your mind. Then you
will be able to test and approve what God's will is—his good,
pleasing and perfect will.

—Romans 12:1–2

The previous chapters provided a way for us to understand some critical aspects of Jesus' character as He walked this earth. However, we cannot stop there on this Jesus Journey. We must now apply the truths we have learned to bring God consciously into our everyday lives.

There are many people who have a great understanding of the first three parts of this book, who have never dared to have an authentic experience of Jesus in their journey of life. It is like saying "I know the ocean well" just by standing on the shore and looking at it. It is not until you feel the waves around you, and dive and see the wonders of underwater life, that you can really say you have experienced the ocean. You can read a million books about how to drive a car, but your ability to drive is only gained by getting behind a steering wheel and turning on that ignition. Until those car wheels start to roll and you put that car into gear and press on the gas pedal, your head knowledge of driving cannot give you the practice you need to be a proficient driver.

It is the same with God.

Jesus is desperately seeking those who want Him beyond the pages of the Bible, who seek to love God with all their hearts, souls, strength, and minds (Luke 10:27). This requires having put into practice a life of communion and dependence on God's truth. So how can we go about applying the truth of His word into our lives?

There are some parts of the Bible you can fly right on by and not realize the importance of a specific section or verse. When Jesus asked His disciples "Who do you say I am?" Peter answered correctly by declaring, "You are the Christ" (Matthew 16:15–17, ESV). Jesus then said that it was God who had revealed this eternal truth to Peter.

Now, we live in a world where Christ has been watered down to, at best, a sweet little baby in a manger, a good man, a teacher and at worst a mythical figure from the past. Nothing much is said about the reality of who He is today, let alone who He can be to each of us.

I hope that as we look at Jesus' potential importance and preeminence in our lives, God reveals the truth of who He really is to us. The fact is, many have gained a head knowledge of who Jesus is but very few have allowed for Jesus to be experienced at the most intimate, vulnerable heart level, which allows His transforming power to be activated and displayed in every aspect of a person's life. So I ask: Who is Jesus to you?

Your Heart's Cry:

Heavenly Father, the eternal question of who You are to me needs to be answered. Your Word tells me that Jesus Christ alone reveals the fullness of God. Everything I need can be found in You, Jesus. You are my Savior, my Peace, my Healer, my Comforter, and more than can ever be written or said. Today my heart cries out, "You are the Christ!" Let that eternal truth be displayed in greater measure each and every day of my life until forevermore.

Day 25

YOUR SAVIOR

Hosanna in the highest heaven!

—Matthew 21:9

From childhood, we were regaled with fairytales of gallant princes on white horses who always arrived just in time to save the damsel in distress. And although we all have outgrown our belief in knights in shining armor, we do find ourselves in distress and in need of a rescuer. The good news is that we do have a rescuer who already displayed the most chivalrous and gallant rescues of all time!

"Hosanna" is a Hebrew term which means "savior." Jesus Christ is the One who saves. "Don't trust men and their horses," the psalmist wrote thousands of years ago (see Psalm 20:7), and this advice still rings true today. This world will not deliver you from your struggles—nor will family, friends, government, charities, doctors, or advice from the experts.

Jesus went to the cross and died for you. How much love He must have for us to make such a sacrifice. However, this saving power did not end at our receiving salvation. It is available to us in every part of our lives! Appreciate that reality for a minute and let its divine truth sink into your heart and mind, so your perspective changes from one of constant defeat to absolute victory.

When you cement in your heart that God will deliver you from your troubles by His mighty hand, the quiet trust that surely comes relieves us from our fears and strivings. It is then that you can be still and know that He is God—and that is enough. Enough to forgive you of the mistakes that haunt you and put your life back on the course of purpose and success.

God does not discriminate; there is no sin too big for His saving grace. God does not accept that any situation is too hopeless for Him to come and turn around by His power. Start going against the comfort of doubt and step into the realm of faith. God's saving power is waiting there.

Maybe a tragedy has come upon you that you did not see coming. This can blindside even the most devout followers of Christ. How do we reconcile believing in a loving Savior in such trying times? I have seen persons go through such trials. A dear friend of mine lost her son recently and she was able to comment that God seemed especially close and comforting during that difficult time. Many persons even commented that her strength and perseverance were amazing to see in that dark time. God seems to extend a special grace to those who experience tragedy and turmoil, saving them from falling into despair and hopelessness as they reach out to Him.

Your Heart's Cry:

Lord, You know the situations that are heavy on my heart. The burdens are just too much to carry, Lord. I am so tired, and I have been tired for longer than I can remember. You said now is the time for salvation and You cannot lie. I choose to put away the doubts and go by faith that You are mighty to save. Somehow and some way You will provide the way to escape or to strengthen me through this ordeal. Save me, Lord; come in Your majestic and limitless power and save me! I cry out to You to deliver me and to set my mind and heart at peace.

Day 26

YOUR GUIDE

Trust in the Lord with all your heart and lean not on your
own understanding; in all your ways submit to him, and he
will make your paths straight.

—Proverbs 3:5–6

So many of us have spent our lives struggling to figure out the best
path to take, which option we should choose, and where we should
go. For many of us, we look back with deep regret because hindsight
has made it clear that we chose the wrong ways and that the results were
chaotic, expensive, and damaging emotionally, physically, or spiritually.
Sometimes those bad choices can cost us all these things.

To be fair, we are human, the result being that:

- we have only so much information and cannot see all the available
  options.
- our feelings and emotions sometimes block the reality of a
  situation.
- past experiences may cloud us from seeing the situation for what
  it really is.

Therefore, we must turn to Jesus and rely on Him in all things all the
time. He can make a way where there is no way. As God says to Isaiah:
"For I am about to do something new. See, I have already begun! Do you
not see it? *I will make a pathway through the wilderness. I will create rivers
in the dry wasteland*" (Isaiah 43:19, NLT, emphasis added). The Lord can
give us insight that we may not have seen otherwise. He will help us to

weed out the feelings and lack of insight to give us a clearer picture and ensure that the path we take is ultimately the right one.

Having access to God's wisdom is a wonderful, priceless gift that we should never take for granted. Unfortunately, many of us do. To do so is to be a person sitting next to a river and dying of thirst. But let us end that today. From now on our own reasoning will not be where our decisions begin and end. Let us bring God to the decision table and give Him the place at the head. He says, "Come now, and let us reason together" (Isaiah 1:18, KJV).

Once I was feeling down and depressed that I was not achieving everything I thought I should have by that time. Eventually, I went to God with my head held low, feeling utterly useless and ashamed. In the hopeless state, God said to me: "Cherise, you are doing great. I am proud of your work and excited to see you complete it. Well done!"

You can imagine my shock. God thought my life was going great? I quickly had to ask, "Ummm, Jesus, you do realize that we are talking about *my* life, right?" The truth is we can sometimes judge ourselves too harshly.

On the other hand, we may overlook some serious issues, thinking that they are okay when we really need to address them. His ways are truly not our ways and His thoughts infinitely higher than our thoughts. And that is something we should celebrate and accept every day of our lives. Let Him gently lead you, for He is taking you to His best so you too can reflect and realize that is His way. God's way is always the right way.

Your Heart's Cry:

Lord, You have only the best intentions for my life. Let me not entertain any other perspective or idea but that eternal truth. Every day I know that circumstances and trials will come to make me doubt, but I trust in Your grace to keep my eyes fixed on You. As I do this, I know I will be able to stand strong and make the correct choices every step of the way. Today, I take Your hand and walk confidently into the future with You.

Day 27

YOUR BEST FRIEND

The LORD is compassionate and gracious, slow to anger,
abounding in love.

—Psalm 103:8

S ome of us have experienced the blessing that a best friend can
bring. There is nothing like that relationship of trust which allows
you to express your truest feelings, deepest desires, and fears. It allows
you to be vulnerable because you have the comfort that, no matter
what, this person will be on your side and support you. At least that
is the hope.

Unfortunately, at some point everyone, including best friends, will
disappoint you. Some people have experienced the ultimate betrayal
of friends who broke their trust. Indeed, it may not be anything as
dramatic as betrayal. It could be that your friend simply could not
be there to support or comfort you because of circumstances outside of their control. As great as best friends can be, they have their
limitations.

Happily, Jesus Christ can be the real best friend of our lives. He will
never leave us or forsake us. He is the "friend who sticks closer than a
brother" (Proverbs 18:24). As this verse says, you want someone who is
always available to empathize with your worries and concerns, to provide
comfort, bring reassurance, and lighten the load.

I have had the supreme privilege of having a best friend for more
than thirty years. Juann and I have been through just about every high
and low our thirty-plus years could offer, but one that sticks out for

me was when I suffered a terrible breakup. I was really heartbroken and started to doubt myself. Was something wrong with me? Was I not good enough? Did I do something wrong? I am sure most of us go through this after a relationship ends. When I told Juann about my fears, she was ready to give me back that sorely needed confidence and put away the doubt. Her words were along the lines of: "How dare he break up with you? He should be lucky someone as great as you even considered him in the first place! You were practically doing him a favor dating him! You deserve better anyway! You are too awesome to settle for someone like him!" On and on she went and quite frankly, by the time she was done my confidence was stronger than ever before!

If such a great friend exists in our fallen world, how much more God Himself offers to us! That is why we should take comfort that God is slow to anger when we inevitably make mistakes. I always have this vision in my head when I stumble in my walk with Him that He gently picks me up off the ground and dusts off my knees while He says, "Be careful how you walk, baby." Then takes my hand and we continue along life's journey, our joined hands swinging in happiness!

Ultimately, friendships must be built on love. God provides the love that is patient, kind, and does not envy or boast; it is not proud, does not dishonor others, is not self-seeking or easily angered; it keeps no record of wrongs. God's love does not delight in evil but rejoices in the truth. It always protects, always trusts, always hopes, always perseveres—and it never fails (1 Corinthians 13:3–8).

Your Heart's Cry:

Lord, You are the ultimate best friend and the one I can trust with my deepest secrets and desires, without fear that You will reveal them. I know that You will always be here and never disappoint me in any way. You can fill every void within my life better than anyone else ever could. Come fill the empty spaces in my heart, Lord; be the supernatural, eternal, and faithful friend You are so earnest in promising to be from today. I promise to be honest and vulnerable to You because You come with a heart of compassion, love, and understanding. I will bare all to You because You will lift me up so I can stand strong. I am excited to start our friendship, Lord.

Day 28

YOUR BROTHER

For those God foreknew he also predestined to be conformed
to the image of his Son, that he might be the firstborn among
many brothers and sisters.

—Romans 8:29

There is little else as strong as the ties that bind family. The old adage that "blood is thicker than water" can easily be applied to our Savior, who literally gave His blood for our acceptance into God's family. What a priceless sacrifice for our inclusion as heirs with Him to all of God's kingdom.

When we speak of brothers in this way, we appreciate that we are not considering familial ties of a physical nature. It is not a brotherly relation from natural descent. Jesus made a clear distinction of who is part of the family of God. In Matthew 12:50, He said, "For whoever does the will of My Father in heaven is My brother and sister and mother."

We are not naturally a part of God's family, so to become a "brother" of Jesus we need to be brought into that relationship by God. We are accepted into the Beloved (Ephesians 1:6). Jesus purchased a family with His blood, and so the Bible says: "Both the one who makes people holy and those who are made holy are of the same family. So Jesus is not ashamed to call them brothers and sisters" (Hebrews 2:11).

Of all the people we know, siblings tend to know the most about our character—the good, the bad, and the downright ugly. We tend to be more ourselves around our siblings because, unlike our friends, they can't get rid of us because the relation by blood is undeniable and irreversible. My oldest sister has a great gift of being succinctly honest yet diplomatic—she will tell you the truth of the situation and the correctness of your attitude from a sincere desire to see you be the best you can be.

Like my oldest sister, eldest siblings usually carry that inherent trait of leadership and being able to get all the younger siblings in order. Jesus is our older brother, "the faithful witness, the firstborn from the dead" (Revelation 1:5). Romans 8:29 further confirms this: "For those God foreknew he also predestined to be conformed to the image of his Son, that he might be the firstborn among many brothers and sisters." So, we can confidently believe that Jesus is the big brother of all of us who "were dead because of your sins and because your sinful nature was not yet cut away. Then God made you alive with Christ, for he forgave all our sins" (Colossians 2:13–14, NLT).

The experts say eldest siblings usually carry traits of being excellent role models to the younger siblings. Hence, Jesus is the ultimate eldest brother, who we should always look up to and emulate.

Your Heart's Cry:

Lord, I am welcomed by Your grace into the Beloved. I have been seated in heavenly places with You and I am a coheir with Christ Jesus. What an immeasurable honor and blessing You have bestowed upon us. Jesus is the firstborn and our older brother, and as such You sent Him to be the model for us to follow. He lived a life of complete submission and I want to do the same. Lord, by the grace of Your Spirit give me the desire to function as He did on the earth. I am royalty and as such I have been elevated to the highest position, so let my thoughts and actions represent the selfless, sinless, and committed calling as Your child in the earth. It is a privilege to be called child of the Most High. Let me never take it for granted by reminding me of who I am in You every day.

Day 29

Your Redeemer

God made him who had no sin [Jesus] to be sin for us, so
that in him we might become the righteousness of God.

—2 Corinthians 5:21

Redemption is the act of repurchasing something that was previously
sold. Jesus Christ purchased a remnant of people who, once they
believed in His sacrifice on the cross, were bought with His sacrifice and
brought into the kingdom of God. God saw you and me in our imperfect
and sinful state as worthy of redemption, with the highest price being
paid for us. How great and merciful our heavenly Father is!

Any time the enemy comes to make you doubt your value with the
lies of "you are not important, not good enough, not deserving" and so
on, reject those lies with the truth: The God of the universe chose to hang
on a cruel cross because you are of great and limitless worth to Him. Let
the cross always be a welcome reminder of your redemption cost—it was
immeasurably high, but God said you were worth it!

Without a doubt, we were all the proverbial lost sheep that went
astray but God came looking and was relentless in His desire to bring us
back into His fold. And yet, the blessing of salvation is only the beginning, the tip of the iceberg of the wealth of blessings that are accessible
as children of the Most High. The righteousness of God is bestowed on
every believer so that all the rights of heaven are ours to claim. Every
single one of God's blessings—provision, health, power, wisdom, favor,
joy, and peace, just to name a few—are absolutely yours because of what
Jesus did on the cross. There is nothing more that you or I can ever do

to receive His grace. It is available because Jesus has already done everything. He has once and for all paid the redemptive price.

Unfortunately, there are many who are still trying to earn God's acceptance and think their works will access God's divine grace. What a tragic misconception that is. To do that would be akin to your friend paying for the meal and you going to the cashier and demanding to pay the bill again! That would be silly. We must ensure that we maintain a truthful perspective of what God has done, or we can quickly find ourselves taking up a yoke of slavery that was never intended for us to bear. Remember, Jesus said, "my yoke is easy and my burden is light" (Matthew 11:30).

Your Heart's Cry:

Heavenly Father, You make the crooked places straight and the rough places smooth. You turn the darkness into light. I want the dark places within me to be filled with Your light. I want the sins of my past wiped clean once and for all. I want to turn from my own crooked and disastrous path toward the straight one that leads to righteousness, joy, and peace. I receive Your redemption by faith knowing You are merciful, gracious, slow to anger, and abounding in steadfast love for me. Fill me with hope by pouring Your love into my heart today and always.

Day 30

Your Provider

Consider the ravens, for they neither sow nor reap; they have
no storeroom nor barn, and yet God feeds them; how much
more valuable you are than the birds!

—Luke 12:24 (NASB)

We have the wonderful reassurance that God will always keep His covenant to be our Provider. What reassurance that we do not need to depend on anything or anyone but God for our provision!

Years ago, God told me He wanted me to move away from my family for a time so he could draw me unto Himself. This was all well and good, but I really did not have the money to rent or buy furnishings and appliances for an apartment. One evening, I was passing through a particular neighborhood and He said to me: "You are going to live in there." The next day, I was by my friend's desk at work; I told her God wanted me to move, and casually opened the paper to the classifieds. It was as if this one particular apartment jumped out at me because it said "fully furnished," and the rental price was not as outrageous as the others. I turned to her and asked where this place was, and she described the same area God had pointed out to me! I went the next day to view the apartment with the landlord, along with another potential tenant who was also keen on the place. The landlord said she would get back to us on who she would choose. Later she said to me that she chose me because when she was considering the both of us, she heard a voice say, "Choose the lady." I had my apartment, fully furnished, and at a good price too!

However, there was still a problem. I had to make the deposit plus the first month's rent and I did not have the money. So what happened?

I got an unexpected raise and promotion at my job. In addition, the position was backdated to start from the beginning of the month, even though we were almost at the end of it—that meant the increase included the amount to cover the deposit and first month's rent! Also, the salary increase gave me more wiggle room in my budget, since I would now be having the extra monthly expense of rent.

There are too many stories of divine provision I could tell from my own life and that of other believers' testimonies I have heard over the years. When God has called you to do something, He has already gone before you and made a way. His unconditional promise is this: "And this same God who takes care of me will supply all your needs from his glorious riches, which have been given to us in Christ Jesus" (Philippians 4:19, NLT).

Your Heart's Cry:

Sometimes, Lord, I worry about provision. I worry that I may not be able to meet my needs. On days like that, when the loss of my job threatens, my bills seem insurmountable, and the money runs low, remind me that You are my Provider. My provision is not from my job or my business. My provision is from You. I will work as unto You with no fear, because if You provide for the ravens, Lord, then I know that You are more than willing and able to provide for me.

Day 31

YOUR LOVER

Love never fails.

—1 Corinthians 13:8

As mentioned earlier, love and trust go hand in hand. God's love for us goes beyond tender feelings. His is a commitment to the point of incomprehensible sacrifice.

Some people struggle to believe that God can supply all the love they could ever need; they don't think they can trust Him unreservedly. After all, they have experienced much heartbreak from loved ones before, and they project that lack of trust unto God's character as well.

This outlook brings us all to the inevitable question: Can God really be trusted? This is a reasonable human consideration, since we use what we know to understand that which we do not know. Unfortunately, our point of reference is usually very distorted. To avoid this downfall, the best point of reference we can and should use, when considering if we can trust God with abandon, is to look at how He has shown his limitless love to us.

Let us turn our attention to Jesus' crucifixion. Jesus' suffering of whipping and death on the cross was not only painful on the physical level but emotionally and spiritually as well. Many people place emphasis on the physical pain Jesus went through on the cross. The movie *The Passion of the Christ* showed it in a glaringly raw and dramatic fashion. However, to understand God's sacrifice for mankind, we must go further than the physical.

Jesus experienced betrayal, denial, abandonment, and rejection in a matter of days—following the highs of His triumphant entry into Jerusalem only days before. He was sitting with persons who professed unerring loyalty to death but who, in a matter of hours, scattered like mice at the first sign of opposition. He saw Peter openly deny their friendship three times. We know of Judas' ultimate betrayal for those silver coins. In addition, the backlash of the people calling him King of the Jews then demanding His crucifixion would give anyone serious anguish and heartbreak.

From the moment of Jesus' arrest up until His death, He was completely abandoned by most of His closest friends, betrayed by His disciples, scorned by all, convicted to die by those He lovingly created, and then condemned to die the most humiliating of deaths. The emotional toll must have been enormously devastating. Finally, He also took on all the sins of the world on that cross—past, present, and future, even though he was the Sinless One. He never lied, stole, committed murder, engaged in sexual immorality or the like, and yet He took it on Himself so we could be made clean. The spiritual burden of mankind's entire rebellion is beyond imagining. And He endured all of this just to save you.

We have learned that love is only fuzzy feel-good feelings, but can we rewrite the script on what true love is? True love—the love that only God can give—is so powerful, so committed, so sacrificial that it transcends feelings and desires to give you the best: Himself. Jesus sacrificed everything—heaven, power, authority, position, eternity, dignity, pride, comfort, health, peace, and joy—to take on every form of suffering, even death on a cross, to save His precious ones (Philippians 3:8).

The cross is what true love looks like: a cross with a broken body, bleeding pitifully for the hearts of men who boldly despised him. That is the love that has come after you and brought you to this point in your life. It is that love that wants to hold you close and take you lovingly through life's journey of spiritual discoveries in Him. It is a life that can never be fully understood, but it can be fully accepted.

Compassion for you kept Jesus committed to making that ultimate sacrifice. We are that precious to Him. Because to God, you and I are simply worth it.

Your Heart's Cry:

Lord, with a sincere heart I want to truly love You. You have shown me what love is; it is willing to go as far as it takes to protect another. It is willing to be vulnerable to being rejected but still opening Your heart to give out compassion without any reservation or self-preservation. I, in turn, want to open my heart to receive that love continuously. I want to know what it is like to live a life of limitless love that brings freedom and victory. I know it is in that place of honor that a dormant love within me will be awakened to know You and the hope of Your calling.

Day 32

YOUR SONG

The LORD your God wins victory after victory and is always with you. He celebrates and sings because of you, and he will refresh your life with his love.

— Zephaniah 3:17 (CEV)

Here is a testimony of the power of God! God had told me to add this chapter title to the book, but somehow I forgot. I was listening to my iPod one night as I was wrapping up my writing, and then I heard God say, "Go to the other song." It seemed like a strange request, but I did it. It started with a man talking and I could not even remember what the song was. The song was "You Are My Song" by Fred Hammond and Radical for Christ. The singing soon began, and the song's lyrics serenaded about God being our symphony and melody forever. It then came back to me that I was supposed to write a chapter with this title!

Isn't it amazing that God would remind me and even provide the inspiration through that very appropriate song, which I had honestly forgotten was on my old iPod?

And there is more. After playing this song a couple times, my iPod died. Since I was now too wired to go to sleep, I decided to pick up my tablet and read the Bible in the meantime. I asked God to give me direction on what to read, and I felt His still small voice in my spirit say, "Psalm 92." I had no clue what the psalm was about, but God and I were on a roll that night and I was going to be obedient.

Here are the words that greeted me: "It is good to praise the LORD and make music to your name, O Most High . . . to the music of the ten-stringed lyre and the melody of the harp. For you make me glad by your deeds, LORD; I sing for joy at what your hands have done" (Psalm 92:1, 3–4). By this time my mouth was literally hanging open. I looked up and said, "Okay, God. I am getting a little freaked out here!"

The power of music is littered through history. Every culture has music, and the majority use instruments to keep beat and time. Music is an elemental need for the human psyche that can transcend differences in language and culture.

It has been said that a more accurate version of "God spoke" in Genesis at the beginning of creation is actually "God sang." The universe sings of the glory of God, and God in turn sings over each us! You don't believe me? God's Word says it: "You are my hiding place; you will protect me from trouble and surround me with songs of deliverance" (Psalm 32:7).

God sings of His love for us continuously, and He wants our hearts to be so filled with His love that we sing of our love right back to Him. God is the original Soloist, and His harmonies and melodies not only sang the creation into the universe but sings over each of us now and forevermore (Zephaniah 3:17). A majestic melody from the heavens is constantly being sung over you every moment of every day. How wondrous are the melodies of God's love. Say it with confidence when you feel the need to hum or sing out to God: you are God's song and He is yours!

Your Heart's Cry:

Lord, You have been singing songs of love and deliverance over me all my life. Let me hear Your song in everything around me. As I rest in You, give me songs of rejoicing and put Your sweet melodies of love in my heart. Lord, I want to sing to You songs of worship, honor, and joy. As I lift my voice to You, let me feel Your pleasure in my spirit, Lord.

Day 33

YOUR ENCOURAGER

I keep my eyes always on the LORD. With him at my right
hand, I will not be shaken.

—Psalm 16:8

I remember a few years into my spiritual walk with the Lord, when
I kept allowing the guilt of my past to tarnish the present relationship I was trying to build with Him. One day God spoke to me while
giving me a vision: "My darling child. This is how you see yourself." At
that moment the vision showed a figure who had a cloud of dark gloom
around her, no light, and she was clothed in horrible gray rags, tattered
and dirty. Her head and back were bowed so low you could not even see
her face, and her silhouette reflected her low self-confidence and sadness.
Seeing the vision made me terribly sad because it was true. I did not feel
worthy of God's love.

Then God said, "Now this is how *I* see you." At once, the vision
changed and there was bright light all around and then a figure appeared
through the light. There was another woman, but this time her radi-
ance was almost blinding. Her clothes were opulent, gold, with innu-
merable adornments and on her head was a beautiful crown. Her hair
was a beautiful afro, glistening resplendently in the light. What was most
fascinating was her stance, her smile and her eyes. Her demeanor was
one of happy confidence, a person who knew she was deeply loved and
her demeanor showed it. Her smile was the most genuine one I have ever
seen. She didn't look shrouded in the guilt of her past sins and mistakes.
She looked as if sin and adversity had never tarnished her life. Her eyes
were filled with a kindness and joy that I now understand comes from

knowing you have such a wonderful support system in Christ; when His encompassing love has filled you so completely and it reflects in your eyes. All this spilled from within her because the windows are the eyes to the soul and reflect what is in them. In her was joy from knowing who God is and truly experiencing the wonder of Him in a real way.

From that day on, I used that vision to transform how I viewed myself, and it also helped me to approach God with confidence.

Somewhere along the line, some of us have bought into the lie that God is this big, horrible master who is just waiting for us to mess up so He can crush us. We must throw away this horrible notion like yesterday's news! For on the contrary, He is so willing to remind us of His love and best intentions for us that He inspired the Bible's writings as a constant reminder of His eternal commitment to see the best being realized in our everyday lives.

Your Heart's Cry:

Heavenly Father, there are many in this world who give some form of encouragement to others. However, I don't want to miss out on being connected to the true source of encouragement—You. You have blessed Your people with a book filled with limitless promises. The blessings of the Lord are a constant source of encouragement, Lord. Let me never forget that and come to that source daily to remind myself that You are my encourager now and forever.

Day 34

Your Judge

I do not even judge myself. . . . It is the Lord who judges me.

—1 Corinthians 4:3–4

As great as all the previously mentioned facets of Jesus' character are and always will be, it would be remiss of me if I did not ensure we have, and continue to keep, a balanced and reverential view of our Lord. Seeing Jesus Christ as the Judge is integral to doing just that. The universal church has been focusing heavily on what I will term the "soft side" of Jesus in modern times, completely different to the fire-and-brimstone style of preaching that was popular centuries ago. It was thought that such aggressive preaching was not as effective as focusing more on the love, peace, and mercy of God. I think each of them has their place, but it needs to be within the right context and understanding of God's true character. It is up to you and me to find the healthy balance between the two.

In the age to come, we will all have to give an account of our lives (Romans 14:12). We each must answer the call and be about our Father's business. To have a skewed and distorted view of the fullness of Jesus Christ will seriously hinder our walk with God and cause us to live far below His potential for us. None of us wants that.

In His sovereign wisdom, God has called each of us to a lifestyle of holiness and love. More than that, He has blessed us with unique gifts to help others make the world a better place and shine our own reflection of God's light. All those are necessary, but today let us take the standard a little further. God calls those who have proclaimed their commitment, to follow His holy standard in every aspect of their lives.

In Matthew 23, we see Jesus openly critiquing the Pharisees as He carries out His ministry. Why was Jesus so harsh to these religious men? After all, He was dealing daily with sinners of all kinds: prostitutes, swindlers, adulterers, corrupt officials, and the like. Why, out of all these people, was He calling out the shortcomings of these pillars of the community?

Let us take a closer look. On the surface, these Pharisees were doing alright. They had the holy talk. They had the holy dress. They frequented the temples. They were diligent in their prayers. They paid their tithes and offerings. They steadfastly studied the Scriptures.

The problem was that it was all a show of self-righteousness. Jesus called them hypocrites, which in that time referred to those who performed in the theatres. The actors would put on masks to pretend to be someone else. Just like the actors, if one looked under the mask, you would see who they really were. In like manner, if we looked past the Pharisees' outer façade, we would see they were prideful, selfish, greedy, power-and status-hungry, legalistic, condescending, and insincere in their faith that was completely without compassion or love. That is why Jesus called us to exceed this type of lifestyle: "For I tell you that unless your righteousness surpasses that of the Pharisees and the teachers of the law, you will certainly not enter the kingdom of heaven" (Matthew 5:20).

To achieve genuine righteousness which Jesus commands us to possess, each of us must allow the Spirit of God to shine the spotlight on our hearts and ask the Holy Spirit to show us those shortcomings. Be it selfishness, greed, rebellion, gossip, pride, unforgiveness, lust, jealousy, or any other sinful practices that we allow in our lives. "The LORD does not look at the things people look at. People look at the outward appearance, but the LORD looks at the heart" (1 Samuel 16:7).

Let each of us humble ourselves and allow the Holy Spirit to reveal our hearts right in this moment—and let it become a daily practice. Let the Holy Spirit clean us up so we won't be those at the end of the age gnashing our teeth because of the many missed opportunities. Let you and I share in the happiness provided to us by being obedient and having tender hearts that hear and follow the Lord's guidance.

Your Heart's Cry:

Heavenly Father, it seems everyone wants to judge and condemn in this world. Thank You that I can trust You to judge accurately the intents of my heart the right way. Today, I present my heart for You to judge. Reveal to me where my shortcomings are—be it fear, unforgiveness, selfishness, greed, or doubt. Strip away the masks I present to the world and sometimes even to myself. Reveal the weaker side of me because I am confident that when I do, Your Spirit will start to transform it into the beauty You intended my heart to be. Thank You for the heart surgery I know You have already started from this moment. I am confident that You who have begun this good work are more than able to finish it. I am excited for this makeover, Lord! I rest in Your judgment with comforting trust because You are carrying me every step of the way.

Day 35

YOUR SAFE HAVEN

And [God's] righteousness will bring peace. Yes, it will bring quietness and confidence forever.

—Isaiah 32:17 (NLT)

I have a nephew who, at the time, was about eighteen months old. When he couldn't see his parents, he became upset. If he was in a room and they left without his knowledge, once he realized they were gone he began to cry until he could find them or they reappeared. When they did, how happy and confident he became again! He knew that with his parents he was safe and secure. In his toddler mind, mommy and daddy were his safe haven.

In Jesus Christ is always a safe place to be. He wants to give us a similar confidence to what my nephew finds in his parents. He wants us to be so secure in His love and His wonderful intentions for us that we constantly seek Him. When we do, we have that assurance that He is right there with us as a constant source of strength, provision, and affection.

There is a famous hymn that says we can hide in the cleft of the Rock. Jesus is the Rock of our salvation. Furthermore, that Rock is where we can go for shelter from life's storms. Do you know that in the cleft of a rock you can find shelter from the greatest hurricanes and storms nature can offer and they will not touch you? No matter how the wind howls and the gusts rage all around, no harm can come to the one who hides in the Rock's crevice.

It makes so much sense then that God, in His infinite wisdom, gave us so many Scriptures about relying on Him:

Cast your cares on the LORD and he will sustain you. (Psalm 55:22)

Take my yoke upon you and learn from me, for I am gentle and humble in heart, and you will find rest for your souls. (Matthew 11:29)

Look to the LORD and his strength; seek his face always. (1 Chronicles 16:11)

Do you not know? Have you not heard? The LORD is the everlasting God, the Creator of the ends of the earth. He will not grow tired or weary, and his understanding no one can fathom. He gives strength to the weary and increases the power of the weak. Even youths grow tired and weary, and young men stumble and fall; but those who hope in the LORD will renew their strength. They will soar on wings like eagles; they will run and not grow weary, they will walk and not be faint. (Isaiah 40:28–31)

So do not fear, for I am with you; do not be dismayed, for I am your God. I will strengthen you and help you; I will uphold you with my righteous right hand. (Isaiah 41:10)

The LORD . . . is the saving refuge of His anointed. (Psalm 28:8, ESV)

The LORD is my strength and my song; he has become my salvation. (Exodus 15:2, ESV)

What a glorious privilege we have as believers. It is truly amazing that we can rely on the Ancient of Days as our shelter, where we can find rest for our souls. We can go and draw from His immeasurable strength to make it through the most difficult and darkest days. We can express our fears and concerns and receive His reassurance in return. What a God!

Your Heart's Cry:

Heavenly Father, let me always remember that You are my safe haven. You are my shelter from life's storms. I will hide in the cleft of the Rock of Ages, knowing Your welcoming arms are always open for me. Thank You for being the One whom I can rely on, no matter what. May Your comforting presence be with me now and always.

Day 36

YOUR PEACE

You will keep in perfect peace those whose minds are steadfast, because they trust in you.

—Isaiah 26:3

Peace. We have felt this feeling at some point in our lives; that feeling
of quiet contentment at a particular point in time. Maybe it was gaz-
ing at the stars on a starry night, a leisurely stroll on the beach, watching
a sunset, or remembering a cherished time from childhood. However, the
peace gained from the Holy Spirit is unlike any peace you can feel in the
natural world.

Jesus said, "Peace I leave with you; my peace I give you. I do not
give to you as the world gives" (John 14:27). It is a peace so hidden in
God that you can be in the midst of chaos, trials, and turmoil and still
feel at peace!

In Acts, Paul and Silas were thrown in a dungeon after being flogged
for preaching the gospel (Acts 16:16–40). What did they do after such
treatment? The Bible tells us they were singing praises and rejoicing even
in their bondage and persecution. The other prisoners were listening.
Can you imagine those other prisoners' shock as Paul and Silas' rejoicing
echoed down the prison corridors to their cells? The other prisoners were
probably wondering if they had gone mad! What persons in their right
mind would be happy in such a state?

Paul and Silas had the assurance of God's love, and the anointing of God's peace must have been so overflowing, that it lifted them far above their circumstances to a place that neither earthly fear, physical abuse, nor emotional turmoil could influence. They were in the cleft of the Rock, and there they dwelled in the spirit of peace. In like manner, your soul can be at rest so that your peace will not be upset by every unfortunate situation, harsh criticism or the uncertainty of life. So how can we experience this peace, no matter the circumstances? As it is written, "There is no one righteous, not even one; there is no one who understands; there is no one who seeks God . . . and the way of peace they do not know" (Romans 3:10–11, 17).

There are two things we need to do to experience peace through Jesus Christ. First, we must be righteous, which means being obedient to the will of God. Isaiah 32:17 says, "The fruit of that righteousness will be peace; its effect will be quietness and confidence forever." Second, to develop true and lasting peace we must seek God through His Word, worship, and prayer. These activities lead us into the very presence of God, and His Spirit will grant us inner peace in abundance!

Your Heart's Cry:

Dear Lord, You said in Your Word that You would give peace to us not as the world gives, which is transitory, shallow, and fleeting. Your peace is a consistent, deep, and eternal one that truly gives rest to our souls. I am eager and open to receive Your peace as I traverse life's journey. I know that once I accept Your portion, I shall not be afraid or troubled, for I trust in You.

Day 37

YOUR SUSTAINER

Surely God is my help; the Lord is the one
who sustains me.

—Psalm 54:4

The enemy always comes with nasty lies. All through our lives we have heard horrible lies such as:

I will always be alone.

I will always be a failure.

I will always be miserable and unhappy.

I will always be unattractive.

I will always be overlooked.

I will always fall short of God's standards.

I will always be addicted to alcohol/pornography/partying/drugs, etc.

I will always be a liar/cheater/gossip/deceiver.

I must compromise my morals to be successful.

I will always be poor and struggling.

These horrible lies are part of the enemy's plan to deceive us into settling for less than God has called us to. The Bible tells us the true intention of our enemy is to steal, kill, and destroy (John 10:10). His aim is for us to live defeated and broken lives. The truth is, God will not withhold anything good from those who walk uprightly (Psalm 84:11). What is it you need today to cancel the lies the enemy has been feeding you?

Do you need to be set free from bad habits? God says, "if the Son sets you free, you will be free indeed" (John 8:36).

Do you need to be healed? God says, "by [Jesus'] stripes we are healed" (Isaiah 53:5, NKJV).

Do you need to be provided for? God says, "[I] will supply every need of yours according to [my] riches in glory in Christ Jesus" (Philippians 4:19, ESV).

Do you question your future? God says, "For I know the plans I have for you, declares the LORD, plans for welfare and not for evil, to give you a future and a hope" (Jeremiah 29:11, ESV).

We are all created in His image and likeness, and He is greatness, so we are called to live in that reality too. You are great. I am great. When we believe and agree with that truth, God can display it in our lives.

Mediocrity is a lie; therefore, settling for less than God's best is not for you. Walk away from the lie and step into the truth; God is waiting for you there.

Your Heart's Cry:

Lord, You want to give me the perseverance to endure the trials of life. I know we live in a fallen world where we are constantly being tested. In order to keep my resolve to trust in Your strength, I need Your help. You are always here, willing to strengthen my heart when the valleys of life inevitably come. It is because of this unchanging truth that I can face the future with confidence. Thank You for Your sustaining power, Lord. In You I place my trust.

Day 38

YOUR GOD WITH YOU

The virgin will conceive and give birth to a son, and will call
him Immanuel [God with us].

—Isaiah 7:14

"He is with me no matter what, and I know that at the end of my
life He'll still be with me. He will gently take my hand and lead
me home." This was once said by a woman who had a nervous break-
down. No one had expected her to recover her sanity or be a functioning
member of society ever again. She said that even in her despair, when she
was on twenty-four-hour suicide watch, God found her and stayed with
her. She was not only able to recover but to encourage others to reach
out to God in their despair, no matter what. She said in a calm and quiet
voice that she had come to no longer regret her past because God had
turned her horrible past into a tool to help others.

Let us consider some others who have abided with Him in doubt
and trial.

- God walked with Noah in the years it took for him to build the
  ark.
- God was with David as he was fleeing Saul in the wilderness.
- He was with Joseph in his master's house and when he was in
  prison.
- He was with Daniel in a foreign land of ungodly rulers.
- He was with the apostle Paul as he encountered much opposition
  while spreading the gospel.

You see, the Bible calls Jesus "Immanuel," which means "God with us." His presence in our lives will never falter and if we reach out to Him, He draws ever nearer—closer than a brother. Jesus is excited to be our focused delight. God wants to dwell within our hearts and walk life's unpredictable journey in step with each of us.

Have you been hurt or made terrible mistakes? Do you have a lot of fear or doubt? Are you stressed? God can take you on the journey of healing, forgiveness, restoration, quiet confidence, and trust, and give you a confidence that you never dreamed you could have.

Your Heart's Cry:

Heavenly Father, I am realizing that this life is ultimately a spiritual journey where I am called to trust You. As I read Your word, I realize that those who trusted in You were never disappointed. I want to have a real relationship so that I can see Your work in my life daily, and I can hear Your voice speaking words of love and reassurance when I doubt. I want to know what Your purpose for my life is so I can successfully complete the work You have for me. I have lived before as though You were not there and that led only to frustration, regret, loneliness, and sadness. But no more. I want to live consistently in Your light. I want to dwell permanently in Your love. I want to rest always in Your peace. Make Your presence so real that my life is now a wonderful adventure in You.

Day 39

YOUR HEALER

The Lord said to Moses, "Make a snake and put it up on a
pole; anyone who is bitten can look at it and live." So Moses
made a bronze snake and put it up on a pole. Then when
anyone was bitten by a snake and looked at the bronze
snake, they lived.

— **Numbers 21:8–9**

Healing—this is one of those aspects of God that I think most
believers struggle with. I know I did. You see, the doctor told me I
was sick. The diagnosis was chronic hypothyroidism, or to put it simply,
an underactive thyroid. Essentially, my body was shutting down because
my thyroid, a gland which regulates most of the body's functions, was
not working properly. The solution was to take medication every day for
the rest of my life. At first, I accepted my state but then I realized I was
accepting the doctor's word over God's. At the same time, I knew how
many sick people there were in the world; why would God heal me out of
all of them? I felt God say to me, "This is not about you versus everyone
else. This is between you and Me."

Whose report was I going to believe? I chose God's! And so, I started
building up my faith with the word God had given me. He had said
He would heal me, so I just had to believe it until He did. I continued
to take the medication prescribed by my doctor, but every morning I
declared: "By His stripes I am healed!" I declared Bible verses about
healing over my life, I asked God to break any family curses that may

have brought this sickness over my life. I played worship music about faith every day. I read Bible verses like this one: "LORD my God, I called to you for help, and you healed me" (Psalm 30:2). So what happened? Of course, I was healed!

That was well over a decade ago, and I am happy to say I am still healthy with no signs of illness! Hallelujah, God is good!

Moreover, God is not only a healer of the body. He is a healer of our minds and hearts. We can meet soul-crushing abuse, betrayals, and disappointments over the course of our lives. It can seem impossible to recover and we tend to become unforgiving, resentful, and harden our hearts. My friends, that is no way to live. Unforgiveness is nothing but a prison sentence that keeps you from living the victorious life God intended for you.

Before God, I held hurts of my past deep in my heart, and looking back it was an awful way to live. In Christ, I allowed God to bring to the surface my pain, and His love restored my heart to a place of forgiveness, freedom, and fearless love.

You know what? God can not only restore you, but make you better than you were before. Oh yes, He most definitely can! Now when people try to hurt me, I no longer feel resentment toward them. I am so filled with God's reassuring love that I don't need them to reassure me or validate my self-worth. Furthermore, I now see them through God's eyes and wonder of wonders, I find myself praying earnestly for the brokenness that drives their actions. I ask God to forgive them and help them see the truth as He once did for me.

My dear friends, God wants to be your healer in every part of your life. Will you allow Him to talk to you, and will you listen to where He plans to heal your body, heart, and mind? It will be worth it!

Your Heart's Cry:

Heavenly Father, I lift my eyes from the pain and hopelessness of my situation, and I keep them on You. I choose to focus on Your healing power through Jesus Christ. Silence my doubts and fears and replace them with Your healing love to restore my heart, mind, and body. You are my Healer, Lord. I trust in You.

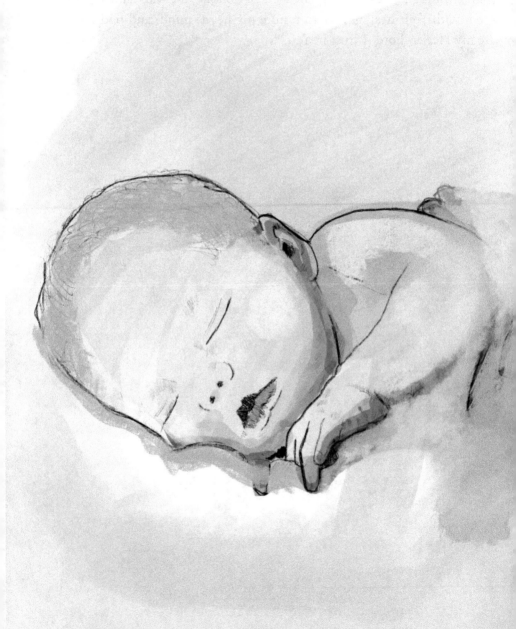

Day 40

YOUR COMFORTER

When anxiety was great within me, your consolation
brought me joy.

—Psalm 94:19

It is always a humbling and amazing fact when we ponder on the reality that we are not only loved by God but that He is eager to take us into His glorious arms and allow us to feel how much He cherishes us. There is nothing like experiencing the realness and potency of Jesus. He desires to constantly lavish us with His peace, joy, and strength. His comfort goes beyond what a close friend, partner, or family can provide.

I can recall one memorable moment when I realized just how seriously God takes His role as Comforter in our lives. I was a new Christian and was living alone at the time. On that day, I felt alone. I said to God something like this. "I feel lonely right now. I could really use a nice big hug right about now." Instantly, I felt a real and tangible warmth encircle me, while a "liquid love" filled me within. God had given me a hug!

Here is a valuable truth: vulnerability is what makes any relationship beautiful. We must all be willing to go before God just as we are. God wants to lovingly guide us to become the best version of ourselves. We can unashamedly be ourselves in His presence because He will clean up the sordid behaviors, shine light on the dark places in our hearts, and show us how to live the best life possible.

Psalm 91:1 says, "Whoever dwells in the shelter of the Most High will rest in the shadow of the Almighty." Likewise, in Psalm 16:11 the psalmist says confidently, "you will fill me with joy in your presence, with eternal pleasures at your right hand."

As we come to the end of this book, I purposely chose Jesus as "Your Comforter" as the last section for a very specific reason. I believe it is one character trait that embodies all God is:

- He comforts us with the promise that we are redeemed and brought into the family of God.
- He comforts us with the promise of eternal life with Him.
- He comforts us when we hurt and are disappointed by the curveballs life can bring.
- He comforts us by showing us the best path to take.
- He comforts us by providing for all our spiritual, emotional, and physical needs.
- He comforts us with His peace when we are tempted to doubt and fear.
- He comforts us by healing our bodies, hearts, and minds.
- He comforts us by constantly reminding us that we are truly loved.

My beloved friend, the Jesus Journey is a personal, passionate, unending, and fully devoted love which is forever ours. Keep walking on that journey, and don't let go of His hand as you do so.

Your Heart's Cry:

Heavenly Father, I need a supernatural Comforter for all that I will encounter in this life. Let me not shy away from Your arms but come running into them daily, knowing that they are always wide open, ready to receive me in Your loving embrace. Lord, You are my Comforter today and always.

For to us a child is born, to us a son is given, and the government will be on his shoulders.

And he will be called Wonderful Counselor, Mighty God, Everlasting Father, Prince of Peace.

—Isaiah 9:6

Contact the Author

Cherise loves to hear from her readers! Be sure to contact her via email at cherisedwiltshire@gmail.com.

CPSIA information can be obtained
at www.ICGtesting.com
Printed in the USA
LVHW012248030921
696923LV00006B/18